Language, Gender, and Sexuality

Language, Gender, and Sexuality offers a panoramic and accessible introduction to the ways in which linguistic patterns are sensitive to social categories of gender and sexuality, as well as an overview of how speakers use language to create and display gender and sexuality. This book includes discussions of trans/non-binary/genderqueer identities, embodiment, new media, and the role of language and interaction in sexual harassment, assault, and rape. Drawing on an international range of examples to illustrate key points, this book addresses the questions of:

- how language categorizes the gender/sexuality world in both grammar and interaction;
- how speakers display, create, and orient to gender, sexuality, and desire in interaction;
- how and why people display different ways of speaking based on their gender/sexual identities.

Aimed at students with no background in linguistics or gender studies, this book is essential reading for anyone studying language, gender, and sexuality for the first time.

Scott F. Kiesling is Professor of Linguistics at the University of Pittsburgh, Pennsylvania, USA.

Routledge Guides to Linguistics

Series Editor: Betty J. Birner is a Professor of Linguistics and Cognitive Science in the Department of English at Northern Illinois University, USA.

Routledge Guides to Linguistics are a set of concise and accessible guidebooks which provide an overview of the fundamental principles of a subject area in a jargon-free and undaunting format. Designed for students of linguistics who are approaching a particular topic for the first time, or students who are considering studying linguistics and are eager to find out more about it, these books will both introduce the essentials of a subject and provide an ideal springboard for further study.

This series is published in conjunction with the Linguistic Society of America (LSA). Founded in 1924 to advance the scientific study of language, the LSA plays a critical role in supporting and disseminating linguistic scholarship both to professional linguists and to the general public.

Titles in this series:

Why Study Linguistics
Kristin Denham and Anne Lobeck

Sign Languages
Structures and Contexts
Joseph C. Hill, Diane C. Lillo-Martin and Sandra K. Wood

Language, Gender, and Sexuality
An Introduction
Scott F. Kiesling

More information about this series can be found at www.routledge.com/series/RGL

Linguistic Society of America

Language, Gender, and Sexuality

An Introduction

Scott F. Kiesling

Routledge
Taylor & Francis Group

LONDON AND NEW YORK

First published 2019
by Routledge
2 Park Square, Milton Park, Abingdon, Oxon OX14 4RN

and by Routledge
52 Vanderbilt Avenue, New York, NY 10017

Routledge is an imprint of the Taylor & Francis Group, an informa business

British Library Cataloguing-in-Publication Data
A catalogue record for this book is available from the British Library

Library of Congress Cataloging-in-Publication Data
Names: Kiesling, Scott F., author.
Title: Language, gender, and sexuality : an introduction /
Scott F. Kiesling.
Description: New York, NY: Routledge, [2019] |
Series: Routledge guides to linguistics | Includes bibliographical
references and index.
Identifiers: LCCN 2018048742 | ISBN 9781138487710 (hardback) |
ISBN 9781138487727 (pbk.) | ISBN 9781351042420 (e-book)
Subjects: LCSH: Communication–Sex differences. |
Grammar, Comparative and general–Gender. | Language and sex. |
Language and languages–Sex differences. | Sexism in language.
Classification: LCC P96.S48 K54 2019 | DDC 408.6/6–dc23
LC record available at https://lccn.loc.gov/2018048742

ISBN: 978-1-138-48771-0 (hbk)
ISBN: 978-1-138-48772-7 (pbk)
ISBN: 978-1-351-04242-0 (ebk)

Typeset in Times New Roman
by Deanta Global Publishing Services, Chennai, India

To Charlie and Emma, my greatest teachers, and to Kim, my newest and most patient one.

Contents

Figures

Acknowledgments

A book is always a work that is accomplished by many more people than the author and contains a multitude of voices. In my case, this list of people started in 1986 when I wandered into a class taught by William Labov and was simply blown away. He showed me how an academic subject can be at once alive, human, socially relevant, and scientific all at the same time. My journey continued from all of my other teachers, including Gillian Sankoff, Ellen Prince, Deborah Schiffrin, Deborah Tannen, Ralph Fasold, Roger Shuy, Heidi Hamilton, mentors such as Walt Wolfram, Barbara Horvath, Christina Bratt Paulston, Alan Juffs, and Barbara Johnstone, fellow grad students at Georgetown and other peers too numerous to mention, lest I leave someone out. I won't go into all the ways that each of these amazing scholars and teachers and friends affected my work, but their voices are all found in this book in different ways.

The voices of my students are here too. I've taught a course in language and gender for more than 20 years, and each group of students was different. I've always taught the class with an approach (in the feminist pedagogical tradition) that encourages the students' own voices and discoveries. It's an approach that tries to meet students where they are and help them through the body of knowledge that exists about the subject so that they can craft their own understanding of it. Along the way, I've learned at least as much from my students as they have from me (actually, I've probably come out ahead). They've put up with my long involved answers to simple questions, digressions that probably only I can see the relevance of, and the fact that I am sometimes simply overwhelmed the multiple and multiplying duties of a professor. They have, without a doubt, had the greatest input to the form and style and content of this book, and if you learn something from this book, you should thank them all.

I wrote the book in a dash, trying to finish before other important events in my life, and as such for a couple of months I was completely consumed by it. This focus affected my wife Kim more than anyone, and there's no way to express the thanks necessary for her patience and encouragement. My daughter Emma was a lifesaver, editing and reading a draft of most of the manuscript. Emma, thanks for all the work; you were a great 'target audience' reader! Finally, I'm sure the voices of all of my family float through the words here; alas, my Dad isn't alive to see the book, but his voice is here too.

This book would not exist without series editor Betty Birner, who not only approached me to write it but also read the manuscript carefully and improved it immeasurably. Lizzie Cox at Routledge has also been invaluable, especially in keeping things on schedule.

Notation and transcription

Linguistics has a lot of specialized notations and ways of representing linguistic things. The most difficult (but useful) is the representation of speech through phonetic symbols. Fortunately, there's a standardization for this in the International Phonetic Alphabet, which I use when necessary but not very much. There's a handy chart relating the sounds to English here: www.antimoon.com/how/pronunc-soundsipa.htm. But that's only English, so there's also this handy chart with links to actual sounds: www.internationalphoneticalphabet.org/ipa-sounds/ipa-chart-with-sounds. I also try to give examples of the sounds in the text by citing words that contain the sound.

Other notations you will encounter:

[tɛkst]	The text in brackets is phonetic notation (IPA).
/t/	A sound (phoneme) in a language, including all the different ways it is pronounced in the language
{-text}	The text is a morpheme. Dashes indicate if the morpheme is a suffix, prefix, or infix.
<text>	The text is an orthographic representation.
(text)	When there is just a short segment in parentheses, this represents a variable in variationist studies (in Chapter 7 primarily).
Text	Text in italics is usually the citation of a word. For example, I might talk about the word *text*, which I am repeating a lot. I sometimes will use italics for emphasis; it should be clear which use is in effect.
Text	Bold words are important terms and key words, which are defined in the neighborhood of their bold use.

Chapter 1

More than talking difference

This book does pretty much what you would expect from the title: It provides an introduction to the relationship between language on the one hand, and gender and sexuality on the other. When you first think of language and gender, you might think of how languages encode gender – things like pronouns and address terms like *Mr.* and *Mrs.* And when you think of language and sexuality, you might think of how sometimes it's possible to guess someone's sexual orientation based on how they talk.[1] While there is a section in Chapter 5 where I discuss each of these ways that gender and sexuality intersect with language, the book is about a lot more than that.

This book is about a wider collaboration between language, gender, and sexuality: Gender is implicated in all the ways that language is used and understood by humans. These connections exist because language is not grammar in a book, nor a dictionary, nor even just the words and rules in your head. Rather, language is inherently a social entity. While we like to talk about languages existing as separate entities, they don't come into being until they are used when people talk (or sign[2] or write) with each other. Moreover, language is something we 'have' as both an individual capacity and a community; your language is partially a capacity of your mind, but it is learned through talking to others. And speakers do more than convey information. For starters, we *do* things with words (as the philosopher John Austin pointed out over half a century ago; Austin 1962): We *order* people around, *request* permission, *insult*, *beg*, *suggest*, and on and on. We also communicate our relationships with people by being, for example, polite or impolite, complimentary, joking, mean, grumpy, cheery, and so on. Finally, you have probably already guessed that language communicates aspects of our identity, for example, in the way you can hear a familiar voice and know who it is just from the voice, or hear a new voice and guess (correctly) something about that person's identity, such as the example above about hearing a voice and guessing that someone is gay. Gender is one of those identity categories that we attach to voices almost immediately. Even more intriguing is that the way we hear voices change depending on what we know about the person. If we expect them to be smart, we are likely to hear language that makes them seem smarter. If we know someone is a woman or a man, we hear their voices slightly differently (see Chapter 7; see also Strand 1999 and Campbell-Kibler 2008).

All of this might make it seem that language simply 'reflects' the social world: We recognize categories of people, and language works in such a way as to reflect those categories. But the relationship between social category and language, as we will see, is much more complicated. Language simultaneously reflects the social world and helps to *create* that social world. In other words, it doesn't just reflect some pre-existing gender categories that are 'out there,' but actually helps to create those categories for communities of speakers. Moreover, speakers use language to signal what they understand about those categories – that is, what they understand to be the kinds of people who are feminine or masculine, what counts as masculinity and femininity, and even whether there are two mutually exclusive categories that exhaustively complete the system of gender categorization.

Language is used by people to do social things in interaction, language is used to reflect the social categories people identify with, and language helps to create and define those very categories. In the main chapters of this book, we'll explore how each of these three processes work with respect to gender and sexual identity. Before we get there, in the next few chapters we'll get some background understandings about theories of gender and about linguistics. Chapter 2 is about language and how linguists study it. You already have a lot of ideas about language before you start studying linguistics, and if this is your first encounter with linguistics, it's important to understand how linguists think about language and approach its study (hint: it's not about telling people how to speak). In Chapter 3, we approach gender, sexuality, and identity as a subject on its own. There are of course whole courses and books and multi-volume encyclopedias devoted to this subject, so it will be necessarily selective and set a baseline understanding for what I mean when I'm talking about these concepts in the rest of the book. The final introductory chapter (see Chapter 5) contains a short discussion and history of the subfield of linguistics called language, gender, and sexuality. It's a wide-ranging field at this point (see, for example, Hall and Barrett in press and Ehrlich et al. 2014), and this chapter will help to situate the field and explain why some things have been studied and some not.

Once we're finished with those chapters and have the foundation laid, we can delve into the particulars of relationships among language, gender, and sexuality in the three main chapters of the book. Chapter 6 explores the ways in which language **creates categories** of gender and sexuality, and the ways that people use language to do that categorization and communicate what they expect people of different categories to be like. Then we turn to **interaction**, and the ways that meanings are created in interaction (also called **discourse** or **conversation**), and how those interactional meanings and moves get connected to gender and sexuality. In the final main chapter, we address the ways in which things like a person's accent are related to their gender and sexual identities, and how these **norms** circulate and are perpetuated (the fields of **sociolinguistic variation** and **perception**). This three-way division into *categorization*, *interaction*, and *variation* is artificial – in real life, people categorize during interaction and relate the categories to the norms and expectations about the people they are talking to all at the same time. So, in the end, I'll try to get you to think a little more about how all of these facets of language and gender/sexuality work together in language.[3]

What this book won't do is exhaustively catalogue all the currents, directions, and literature in language and gender, especially any such research or arguments that aren't in linguistics. It's meant to be a very short, general introduction to give you an idea of what researchers know and what the conversation is like in this field, and especially to provide you with an appreciation of its diversity. In other words, it's meant to be a good starting point for anyone who hasn't studied language or gender/sexuality. I assume that you haven't studied either one. So, if you're a linguist, you might find some of the linguistics simplified, and if you are a gender/sexuality studies person, you'll find the treatment of gender to be introductory for that field. I hope lots of people reading this are neither linguists nor gender studies majors. Whatever your field, I hope there's a fact or question somewhere in this book that inspires you to look deeper and ask more questions about how language, gender, and sexuality are intertwined.

Who's writing this book?

When I read a book, I always have an idea of who the writer is and what, if any, their agenda is. Even in the most dry textbooks, I will often do this (I want to know who is responsible for such aridity!), and I know from experience that especially when people read books about gender, they often guess about the perspective of the author. So I'm here to take some of the guesswork out. If you don't care about my perspective, then you can skip this section. I especially think it's important to say something about who I am because in many ways I am not your typical language, gender, and sexuality scholar; many, if not most, such scholars identify themselves to be in some 'marked' or 'less privileged' social category, especially in terms of gender and sexual identity.[4] So, if I were to categorize myself in terms of such categories, I'd say that I am a White, middle-class, heterosexual, cisgendered, masculine person (or man[5]). It's interesting to note that most of my colleagues in this field of study are somehow *not* one of those categories, and it is also interesting to note that people tend to expect language and gender/sexuality scholars to be either female or 'Queer' or both. My take on why that might be is that gender and sexuality is not something that people in my social identity categories are forced to think about by their social experiences as much as people in marked categories. However, I've always thought about gender, and I've always thought that doing it is difficult to manage. That might seem odd from the White, masculine, cisgendered perspective, but my own research has largely been about how these unmarked categories (like *White* and *masculine*) maintain their unmarkedness and their power, even while so many people in that category don't feel powerful. So my research has in large part focused on White, middle-class, heterosexual men, to see how these categories might actually be relevant to their language use, and to discover how this use maintains their **hegemonic**, or most powerful, position as a group in society. It's not as easy as you might think, even though most people, least of all the men, don't notice most of the interactional effort that it takes. Even though I'm a member of this hegemonic group, I come to this field with a **feminist** perspective, which means that I am sensitive to these power relations and would like in some way to ameliorate the asymmetries of opportunity because of them (I'll discuss feminism more in Chapter 3).

A word on terminology

Terms for groups of people are a fraught minefield from a number of perspectives, not the least of which is that terms for identities and groups often change if members of those groups object to current usage and coin terms that they find better describe who they are. A good example is the term for people we might most accurately term 'American Slave Descendants' (a term introduced by Baugh 1991). This group has been referred to in many ways throughout US history, and there is often disagreement within this community itself about what the appropriate term is (as Baugh's article describes). I've chosen to use the term *Black* (with a corresponding *White*, both capitalized), but none is perfect, because these categories are social creations and they try to put a huge, diverse group of people into one box. For people from a mainly Spanish-speaking cultural background, I'll use the current term *Latinx* in contrast with *Anglo*. *Trans* is probably currently the fastest moving target in this area (I'll just use the term *Trans*, although it is sometimes written trans*), although the acronym for LGBTQIA+ is another fast moving target (with the 'Q' alternately being cited as 'queer' or 'questioning' and the 'A' as 'ally' or 'asexual'). For this latter identity/community, I'll use whatever inclusive term seems best, including 'non-hegemonic sexuality' and simply 'Queer.' I capitalize all of these categorizing terms (Black, White, Latinx, Anglo, Trans, Queer) to signal that I am referring to a named category which has a clearly thought-out referent, with all the problems of such categories, and in the case of 'Queer,' to differentiate it from its use as a slur (the capital is thus a kind of typographical caveat). Finally, we have to think about the terms *male/female*, *woman/man* (and related categories like *boy/girl*), and *feminine/masculine*. These all have implications for how we think about these categories, as I outline in Chapter 5.

If I'm citing another discussion in which a term is used that is different from the one I'm using, I will generally keep the original. I will try to explain my motivation for most terminology along the way. Since this book (and, if you are reading it for a class, the class) is actually about how people make and refer to these kinds of categories, if you have an objection or query about the terms I use, I suggest bringing the issue up with your class or instructor, and have an open and respectful discussion of such ideas and what would be the best way to resolve them for your classroom community or, failing a resolution, at least create an understanding of the complexities of social categorization. The ability to name and categorize is powerful, and that is why it is such a big deal.

Notes

1 Although, as we will see later on, this process is not value-free, as the default is generally to think others are heterosexual unless some cue to homosexuality is present.
2 Signed languages such as American Sign Language are full human languages with complex grammars.
3 Most of the time in the book, I will distinguish between gender and sexuality, but sometimes it's not an important distinction, or it would be awkward, and I still want to make sure to include both of them.
4 *Marked* is a term that we will encounter repeatedly in this book which means that the term or category is somehow less expected than another option in the set.
5 I'll discuss in a later chapter why I prefer *masculine person* rather than *man*.

References

Austin, J. (1962). *How to Do Things with Words*. Harvard University Press, Cambridge, MA.

Baugh, J. (1991). The Politicization of Changing Terms of Self-Reference Among American Slave Descendants. *American Speech*, 66(2):133–146.

Campbell-Kibler, K. (2008). I'll be the Judge of That: Diversity in Social Perceptions of (ING). *Language in Society*, 37(5):637–659.

Ehrlich, S., Meyerhoff, M., and Holmes, J. (2014). *The Handbook of Language, Gender, and Sexuality*. Wiley-Blackwell, Malden, MA; Oxford.

Hall, K. and Barrett, R. (in press). *The Oxford Handbook of Language and Sexuality*. Oxford University Press, Oxford.

Strand, E. A. (1999). Uncovering the Role of Gender Stereotypes in Speech Perception. *Journal of Language and Social Psychology*, 18(1):86–100.

Chapter 2

Studying language

This chapter provides a brief introduction to the 'scientific' study of language. Of course, you already know a lot about language, because you use it, and are using it as you read these words. But what I ask you to do in reading this chapter is to rethink some of your assumptions about language. The most important task is to try to let go of the attachments you might have to ideas about 'good' and 'bad' language. I'll discuss some of the 'myths' about language and languages, and then we'll move on to explore some of the basic facts about language that linguists have discovered. We then move on to see how we can take this more 'objective' perspective into the realm of the critical, where we look at how language and language use is structured to create and maintain power relations. If you have already learned a fair amount about linguistics, you can probably move quickly through the early parts of this chapter, but I don't recommend skipping it altogether because the topic of the book draws from a number of subfields in linguistics and related fields, such as anthropology, which you may be less familiar with.

Important ideas about language

When I tell people that I am a linguist, the reaction is often to remark, "I guess I'd better watch what I say then!" (in addition to asking how many languages I speak or asking about the local dialect). The idea that there are correct ways of speaking, and that most people fall short of perfect correctness, is pervasive, but judging people's language is not what linguists do. Linguists try to figure **why language is the way it is**: Why do humans have more than one language? How do we learn language? Why does everyone sound different? Those are the types of questions linguists try to answer. We also disagree with each other a lot. So it's worth reviewing some of the assumptions/discoveries that linguists and people working in related fields share. My list is based on one created by Daniels (1994), although I have tweaked the language a bit.

Children learn their native language swiftly, efficiently, largely without instruction, and perfectly

A corollary to this principle is that it doesn't matter what your genetic, ethnic, etc. background is, you will learn the languages of your community. Babies and children are amazing language learning machines, who seem to acquire language magically. The people around the child sometimes provide some feedback, but there are many cultures where very little to no feedback is provided in the sense of 'correcting' the child. Nevertheless, by the time the child hits adolescence, they're already perfect language speakers. One of the questions that linguists pursue is, in fact, how this actually happens – what does a child do and pay attention to in order to get to speak language so perfectly?

All language is systematic

Language is not a collection of words, but rather there are rules for putting those words together. Similarly, language is not just a collection of sounds, but rather each language systematically organizes all the sounds a human can make, uses some of them, and ignores others. Note that this idea states "all language" not just "all languages." This means that every kind of language spoken or signed by a human is systematic; if a human is using it, the language has a system. There are lots of other ideas and ideologies that believe that only some languages, especially the 'standard' ones, are systematic and others (often called 'dialects') aren't systematic. But linguists have shown over and over again that all language is systematic. If you can't perceive the system, it usually means that you just haven't discovered it yet because it is so different from your own. It also doesn't matter what mode a language comes in. Most languages are spoken using sound, but deaf communities have developed signed languages which are full languages in their own right, with all the systematic features of spoken languages.

All languages have three major components: a sound system, a vocabulary, and a system of grammar

All languages put these three things together. They systematically decide which sounds (or gestures) that humans can make are important and decide to ignore others. The meaningful sound distinctions that a language makes are called its **phonemes**. (Phonemes are usually written inside slashes, as you will see in the next sentence.) For example, in some languages, a burst of air after a /p/, /t/, or /k/ makes a different word. But in English, it doesn't. Words like *pit* have a /p/ with a burst of air, while words like *spit* don't. If you are a native English speaker, then you probably can't even hear the difference in the way /p/ is pronounced in these two words. But if you are, for example, a Thai, Hindi, or Korean speaker, the burst of air can mean a completely different word. The same works the other way for the English sounds /r/ and /l/, which aren't differentiated in Japanese. If you are a native Japanese speaker, you've probably had to work hard to differentiate these sounds when learning English.

A language then creates systems and rules about which sounds can go next to each other. In English, we don't put /t/ and /l/ together at the beginning of a syllable, but other languages, such as the indigenous Mexican language Nahuatl, do. Some languages don't allow *any* consonants together. It gets pretty complicated, but amazingly enough, we humans have no trouble at all putting the sounds together if we're a native speaker. We call this 'intuition,' which makes it sound kind of like 'magic,' but it's really a tacit knowledge of all of these complex rules.

Once the sounds are put together, we have words, and these words have meanings of different sorts. Of course, different languages have different words based on their culture and how they are used.

You might think that words exist in a dictionary and that's where the meanings exist. But a dictionary really just documents how words are used and roughly what that says about their meanings (this is no easy task!). These words also have different functions – they describe things, actions, or other relationships (these are otherwise known as parts of speech, such as nouns, verbs, adjectives, adverbs, clitics, and so on). Linguists usually talk about these words more generally as **morphemes**, the smallest units of meaning in languages. Some of these are even just one sound segment, such as the plural {-s} in English, and some are whole words, such as {word} (morphemes are usually written inside curly braces).

These phonemes and morphemes have rules for how they can be put together. This is the system of grammar. How do you put that {-s} on a word to indicate plural? When do you pronounce it as a [z] instead of an [s]? (Descriptions of sounds as they are actually pronounced – as opposed to the abstract phoneme – are usually written in square brackets, which is called phonetic notation.) A famous example showing that word order depends on word categories like *noun* and *verb* is that it's perfectly grammatical in English (although it doesn't make much sense) to say "Colorless green ideas sleep furiously," but it's both ungrammatical and nonsensical to say "ideas colorless furiously green sleep." The latter is indistinguishable from a list of words, while the former is a recognizable sentence, even though it doesn't make much sense! The most basic rules have to do with the ordering of things in different categories (this is true for sounds as well – there are certain kinds of sounds which can and can't come before others, and these rules change depending on whether a sound comes at the beginning or the end of a word or syllable). A large part of linguistics is **documenting** what the rules are for different languages. Linguistic theory is basically about what the best system for writing these rules is – that is, a system of rules that can allow all the possible utterances of language but doesn't allow anything that is not a possible utterance.

Everyone speaks a dialect

Much of popular thinking about dialects relates to the idea that they are somehow substandard or 'imperfect' versions of some ideal 'standard' language. So in this view, for example, there is a platonic ideal (sometimes there is even a government or quasi-government body to decide what this way of speaking should sound like), and everyone who doesn't speak that way has somehow learned the language imperfectly. This way of thinking about language is all about the people in charge of deciding what the language should look like keeping their power. It's not a valid description of how language works. The clearest way to see this is that language wasn't even thought about as national or standard until a few hundred years ago, and humans have had language for tens of thousands of years, at least.

So how *do* dialects fit in? Dialects are simply the way people speak, and they're not subordinate to 'standard' languages, but rather 'standard' languages are dialects of the language just as the geographic dialects are. To the extent that anyone really talks that way, standard **varieties** tend to be spoken over a wider geographic area, and their norms are more overtly **prescribed** by schools and publications and dictionaries than other varieties; non-geographic dialects might be spoken by any community or identity group and are sometimes called more generally **sociolects**. The main point is that dialects are absolutely perfect ways of speaking human language, not deficient national languages.

As for terminology, in this book I'll use several different terms for things like **dialect** and **language**. In addition to those two terms, I'll mainly use the more generic ways of speaking and variety. These basically mean some set of linguistic practices that are used together by some set of speakers; there are problems with both terms, but they are as value-free as linguists can get in describing these things (which are, in many ways, imaginary objects).

Speakers of all languages employ a range of styles and a set of subdialects and jargons

This idea is important, because we tend to think of people as speaking a single specific language or dialect, but in reality, everyone commands a range of different ways of speaking, including different languages (multilingualism is actually more the norm in the world than the exception). Some differences can be subtle, such as when I pronounce my vowels in a little more Southern-ish way when I'm in a more relaxed atmosphere or even when I go to states in the south of the US.[1] Speakers recognize that different ways of speaking go with different situations and people they are talking to. So in formal business situations, or classroom talk, speakers very often expect a more 'standard' style of speaking, while in relaxed situations with friends and family – or even with strangers in places that are supposed to be relaxed like parties or bars – using very formal language would sound weird. Some languages encode this more than others, with Japanese having different 'levels' of politeness, but there doesn't need to be explicit rules for this kind of shifting to happen. The most important lesson to remember from this idea is that language is not fixed, and everyone has some kind of variation in their talk (those who don't are the stuff of sitcoms; just look up the character Laurie Bream in the sitcom "Silicon Valley"). In fact, I'm writing in a tone that you may find odd for a textbook, because I'm trying to make it more like I'm having a conversation than giving a dry lecture.

Language change is normal

Language change really, *really* bothers people. You don't have to look far to find examples of people complaining about how "kids these days" are ruining this or that language, or can't speak correctly (for example, look up arguments about how young [teens and twenties] American English speakers use the word *literally* or *like* and you will find laments about how the language is "going to hell in a handbasket"). The thing is, people a generation before said that about the people saying it now. Change is a feature of language, not a bug. It makes language infinitely adaptable to all the new things, ideas, and concepts that humans invent, and it allows creativity and poetry. So, if someone complains that you didn't use *whom*, you can suggest that English has been losing its case-marking morphology for centuries, and it's time they got over it. You could also ask them why they aren't speaking in Shakespearean English if English isn't supposed to change (or even worse, the Old English of *Beowulf*; you could even memorize some Chaucer and just start reciting to them). There's no fixed English (or any other language). It has always been changing and will continue to change.

Value judgments about different languages or dialects are matters of taste

There's no such thing as an objectively 'better' language than another – all languages do what they need to do. If there is a need to communicate something, speakers invent a way to do that. There are certainly things that languages do *differently*, but also things that require more effort to express; to be blunt, every language is 'clunky' at expressing something. And as far as whether one language sounds better than another, well, have you ever had a discussion with someone about some kind of music being better than another? It's pointless, because this is an aesthetic judgement and such judgments are not based on objective criteria.

However, such judgments *can* be based on ideologies about language that circulate in a culture. Many English speakers would argue that French is a beautiful language, but why? Often, it is because they've only heard French in situations where there is something positive about the speaking of French or the person speaking the language (for example, romance). And I've often heard speakers say German is not beautiful, but that is likely to be because of the kinds of situations in which those folks have heard German. But these evaluations are more about the stereotypes that people have about French-speaking *people* or German-speaking *people* than the actual sound of the language (and of course, throughout much of the last century, German was demonized as the language of a national enemy of the US and much of Europe, so one can see how that stereotype developed). If you want to read a study that shows this more clearly with respect to accents of English, read Rosina Lippi-Green's (1997) chapter on the way that Disney characters (especially the villains!) tend to have certain kinds of accents.[2]

Ways of speaking ('dialects' and 'languages') are intimately related to the societies and individuals who use them, and when and where they use them

So when we have a reaction – positively or negatively – to a way of speaking such as a language or a dialect, we are reacting not to the language but to the stereotype about the person. For example, some people in the US think that people with Southern US accents are not as smart as people with standard accents. In reality, there are as many smart people with Southern US accents as there are with other kinds of English accents. But we've been conditioned to think that Southern people are not as smart as non-Southern people. Similarly, New Yorkers are polite in their own way, and are not really rude as a rule (there are plenty of rude New Yorkers, but that's true of every group of people). But people hear a New York accent and think they are talking to someone who is rude. These are not evaluations of the ways of speaking but rather are stereotypes of a kind of language user. It's just the way they speak, and if you grew up where and when they grew up, you'd probably sound the same way, or at least very similar. So, in short, talk is just talk, and the value of it is added by the listener and their stereotypes of the person they are listening to.

Writing is derivative of speech

Sometimes, people think they should say words exactly as they are written (except maybe *psychology* and *knight*). But humans have been speaking for tens of thousands if not over a hundred thousand years (we're not completely certain), while writing has existed for only a small fraction of that time. So, writing is really just a way to try to get our spoken interaction into a form that will last longer than the sound in the air or the sign movements we make. The interesting (or maybe dangerous) thing is that writing then takes on standards of its own, such as spelling or making characters with the right strokes in the right order. Like language more generally, writing is constantly changing, with people spelling things differently (when was the last time you spelled it 'doughnuts?'). And most recently, we have added emoji to the writing repertoire (although in some ways it goes back to the beginning of writing, using pictures). These emoji have taken on a life and meaning of their own, but originally, they were invented so that some more emotion could be injected into written communication such as texting (☺ starting life as :)). Emoji have made texting much richer, but the need for them points to what is lost in transferring speech to writing.

Questions linguists ask

So, if linguists don't tell people how to talk, then what do they do? As mentioned previously, one thing linguists try to do is find languages that aren't documented and document them. Documentation is particularly important right now, as many small languages are ceasing to be spoken in their original communities (or the communities are ceasing to exist). If the language is documented, it can be revitalized, and linguists are involved in revitalization efforts as well.

Theoretically, linguists ask different questions depending on which subarea of language they work in, but the main idea is essentially to figure out how human language works. So, what are the possible ways that sounds can be organized in a language? Why do some languages organize sounds one way and some don't care about the same sounds? How, in what order, and with what variation are words put together? What are the universal possibilities for the ways that human languages can organize words? If all languages are learned from the same starting point (that is, as a baby and knowing no language), how are our brains set up to learn something so complex so quickly? These questions all share the goal of trying to figure out how our so-called 'universal grammar' is structured. There are a lot of theories for how to do this, but they all share this focus on the general nature of the human language faculty.

There's another school of thought that argues that the way language is structured is related to the way it is used and the kinds of information it communicates, and not simply the way humans are genetically predisposed to learn it. For example, there's a tendency to put information that listeners might already have access to at the beginning of the sentence and newer information later in the sentence. For example, we say something like "Yesterday I saw a cat in the garden. It was blue." If we want to put blue earlier in the second sentence, we have to do a lot of work (and sound like Yoda): "Blue, it was." This pattern is neither universal nor always true, so then things get complicated again. We'll see gender enter into this idea that language use affects grammar, mainly in how and whether gender gets encoded in language.

So, on one hand, linguists try to figure out how all languages are similar (Universal Grammar). But they also ask questions about why all languages are different, and why there's so much variation in languages, why everyone has a slightly different way of speaking, and why languages keep changing to be more different. The last few questions are particularly puzzling. If you were going to design a communication system, wouldn't you have everyone speak the same language? This mystery is the focus of the story of Babel in the Book of Genesis when God makes everyone speak a different language in order to make it harder for humanity to work together and build a tower to heaven. So the question of why humans speak different languages is pretty old, although it does have a few likely answers. The main reason for variation, as you may have guessed, is that languages change, but not in the same way in every community, so that different ways of speaking diverge to the point that people can't understand each other any longer. The big question is why does language change in the first place, and how do those changes spread through a community of speakers? (It's not like everyone who speaks a language suddenly gets a wireless upgrade.) These questions are some of the oldest in linguistics, and we are still fleshing out the answers. We'll address this in Chapter 7, where we look at the role of gender in language change.

Linguists also analyze speech as it is used in interaction, which is the domain of the subfields of pragmatics and discourse analysis. Here again, there are principles that govern the ways that people use language. For example, when there is a choice in how to form a sentence, what reason might speakers use to choose one sentence over another? Politeness is an example of one reason – we'll focus on the study of politeness in Chapter 6 – because it plays into gender significantly.

This discussion has really only scratched the surface of all the smaller questions that linguists get involved in, but it gives you an idea of the big questions they worry about. These issues are also those that are focused on language as an abstract object of study. There are also linguists who study how language is enmeshed in human sociocultural systems, and how it is related to the ways that power and privilege are distributed in these communities, which I turn to next.

Critical linguistics

So, while some linguists study language as a system of its own, others are more critical. No, they're not critical of languages (remember, we linguists love them all). Rather, critical linguistics is about looking at how power relations in society are created and reinforced through language, either through ideologies about language or through the very processes of how language is used. Since this is a book about language, gender, and sexuality, you can guess that one dimension where critical linguists work is in gender and sexuality, and we'll get to that in the next couple of chapters.

One of the important areas of focus for critical linguists is on **linguistic discrimination**. This kind of discrimination does not seem to carry as much stigma as other forms of discrimination. I alluded to such discrimination above when suggesting that people think that speakers with Southern accents are somehow less smart than people who speak in other accents. Linguistic discrimination is pervasive, because it is baked into most education systems. It is discrimination that is not merely about language, but, as noted above, is about what ways of speaking say about the speaker. This connection between a way of speaking and an identity usually has to do with class, race, and native speaker status. Critical linguists try to show how sociolinguistic processes maintain the privilege and judgement around standard language.

One way to combat this bias is through popular education, and such projects are also part of critical linguistics. A great example of this work is the collection of films produced over the years by Walt Wolfram, whose most recent film is *Talking Black in America* (Wolfram et al. 2018). The idea is to communicate much of the information in this chapter (such as language change being normal and judgments about varieties being judgments about their speakers) in a way that is accessible and that people can relate to – especially about the systematic nature of all language varieties and the idea that linguistic discrimination reflects discrimination of a language variety's speakers.

There are also studies that show how much **implicit bias** there is in the relationship between a speaker's appearance and how people hear language, something that is often called **reverse linguistic stereotyping**. As Kang and Rubin (2014) explain, "it is possible that when listeners harbor stereotypes about speaker identity or ethnicity, they may not be able to objectively hear – much less evaluate – speakers whom they believe to speak with an accent," so that "[n]egative expectations about speakers can lead to inaccurate judgments of proficiency." Rubin (1992) outlines a study in which he played the same lecture, originally recorded by a native speaker of 'standard' American English, but told different listeners that different people were giving the lecture, including non-native speakers from different countries. Speakers perceived the lectures of non-US speakers to be worse than those of US speakers, even though it was actually the same lecture.

Finally, some critical linguists try to figure out how language itself subtly but powerfully reinforces stereotypes and ideologies of inequality. There is a wide variety of approaches that are called **Critical Discourse Analysis** (or CDA for short). One approach, initiated by Norman Fairclough (1992), is widely followed, and in large part relies on looking at how people have to rely on ideologies of inequality to make sense of conversations. As we'll see in Chapter 6, one of the mysteries about interaction is how people actually manage to have coherent conversations even though there isn't a 'script' for how to have each individual conversation. This coherence is partly created by relying on what we might think of as 'background knowledge.' This background knowledge is actually structured by ideologies, especially social ideologies. For example, imagine a police officer asking a suspect, "When did you stop doing drugs?" or "How many drinks did you have tonight?" They are assuming that the suspect has at some time been doing drugs or that the suspect has had at least one drink. This kind of critical linguistics is important in language, gender, and sexuality research from a feminist perspective, since the goals of feminism include highlighting and ameliorating power differences that are related to gender.

This has been a very small sampling of all the linguistics research that goes on. As you can see, as language is systematic on its own, sometimes it can be studied without reference to the people who use it. But because language is also a social tool, it can be studied critically to look at how language and social identities and power are organized.

Notes

1 I'm not actually from an area that people would call the South, but in fact the speech in Southern Indiana is in a dialect area often referred to as the "Hoosier Apex," which has a lot in common with the dialect in Kentucky, which people would call "The South."

2 Linguists are not immune to this either. We love all languages, but we do have aesthetic reactions to some ways of speaking. Hopefully, we understand where they come from. Personally, I love the sound of Portuguese, but I suspect that has to do with my hearing it being sung in jazz tunes that I particularly like.

References

Daniels, H. A. (1994). Nine Ideas About Language. In Clark, V., Eschholz, P., and Rosa, A., editors, *Language: Readings in Language and Culture*, pages 18–36. Macmillan, New York, NY.

Fairclough, N. (1992). *Discourse and Social Change*. Polity Press, Cambridge, MA.

Kang, O. and Rubin, D. (2014). Listener Expectations, Reverse Linguistic Stereotyping, and Individual Background Factors in Social Judgments and Oral Performance Assessment. In Levis, J. and Moyer, A., editors, *Social Dynamics in Second Language Accent*, volume 10, pages 239–254. Mouton de Gruyter, Boston, MA; Berlin.

Lippi-Green, R. (1997). *English with an Accent: Language, Ideology, and Discrimination in the United States*. Routledge, London; New York, NY.

Rubin, D. L. (1992). Nonlanguage Factors Affecting Undergraduate's Judgments of Nonnative English-speaking Teaching Assistants. *Research in Higher Education*, 33:511–531.

Wolfram, W. (Producer), Hutcheson, N. (Director), and Cullinan, D. (Director). (2018). *Talking Black in America*. [Motion Picture]. The Language and Life Project, Raleigh, NC.

Chapter 3

What are gender and sexuality?

A short introduction to a very big topic

Gender is the second word in this book's title, so let's explore just that concept. This discussion will be very brief; there's no way to engage with all the issues surrounding gender in a single *book*, let alone a short chapter. Gender is a difficult subject, partially because it is so hard to actually define, and partially because it is a concept that consistently gets redefined. (To make matters worse, it is something that every human engages with on a daily basis.) If you look for discussions of 'gender' in English before the 1970s, you won't see much except for discussions of grammatical gender in languages. That's because before that time *gender* wasn't used to refer to the social category, but rather was seen more as an essentialized biological category. In fact, Baker (2008) cites Money (1955) as the first use of *gender* to mean something like an "identity based on biological sex." It wasn't until feminist theory started to point out the socially constructed nature of gender (and sex, for that matter) that the word started to be used more widely to refer to the (usually binary) categorization of people based largely on their perceived reproductive capabilities. Before the shift to understanding gender as socially constructed, gender was referred to as *sex*. As gender has become the more dominant term over those decades, *sex* has come to be used almost exclusively as part of a compound verb for the act of coitus (*have sex*) and related derived nouns (as in *sex education*). One of the most common distinctions you'll see between sex and gender is that *sex* is the biological category assigned at birth, while *gender* is the social patterning based on that biological base (see, for example, Rubin 1975). This use keeps, to some extent, the original use of sex to divide humans by genitalia, hormones, and so on.

But now *gender* is used almost exclusively for the binary division of humans. There are many definitions of gender, and many people don't define it but follow the famous maxim that "I know it when I see it." Somewhat like language, gender is a combination of the individual and the social, and can't exist without some part of both. Further, the terms are a definition of a structural system: that is, *femininity* is defined in part by not being *masculine*, and vice-versa. For that opposition, a larger group of people is needed. Most of us fill out forms (or, when we were born, had one filled out for us) that classifies us according to gender, usually using the terms *woman/girl/female* or *man/boy/male* (or the rough equivalent in another language). This makes it look like gender is some sort of fixed attribute we were born with and carry around with us, much like eye color (which, you might note, is also probably on your driver's license with height, gender, and possibly hair color). So, while it seems like gender is an individual attribute, it is the system of social categorization that makes it possible.

All of this talk of gender categorization might seem obvious, and you might wonder why we are talking about it, but humans don't really *have to* make such a big deal out of gender. The only time gender is really unavoidable is when we want to make new humans – we need something from male biology and something from female biology (even though these days we can get the building blocks without actual coitus, but we still need a human womb, which not all of us have). It is possible to imagine a world (although it might be hard) in which everyone has no gender, and baby-making is a minor and relatively insignificant part of one's life. But, of course, we *do* make a big deal out of it; it's one of our most basic and universal ways of sorting people out, and that sorting has consequences for how people live their lives. Not only that, we work really, really hard to display our gender, usually elaborating the differences as much as possible, even when it's not needed (or wanted). Women have surgery to increase bust size, while men lift weights to increase muscle mass (among other anatomical sizes that men obsess about). This gender difference privileges some and disadvantages others. It can restrict what kinds of life courses are open to people of the different categories and even affect what kinds of activities and personalities they *want* to have.

So, gender is a lot more than a person's individual biology. Well then, what is it? Is gender some sort of *attribute* of a person, attached to and part of them? If so, then what are the possible attributes, and why those attributes? Gender is comprehensive – a system that involves an individual, their habits (including speaking), their feelings, and how they experience the world. But it's also involved in more collective human aspects such as economies, nations, and institutions like families. Gender is not located in one place, then, but is an aspect of human existence that suffuses itself through most aspects of our lives.

Gender even gets attached to non-animate things. For example, I was once driving with my son, about ten years old at the time, who noted that a particularly large vehicle was *masculine*. Then he said, "How can a car be masculine? What makes it masculine? It's not a person or even an animal." (Children are often the most astute social observers!) Indeed, how can a car be masculine? This question points out that beyond the personal and societal sorting work that gender does, it is also (perhaps primarily) an **ideological system**. An ideological system, also just called and **ideology**, is a shared conceptual system for organizing the world. Not everyone who shares the ideology – in the sense that they are aware of it and can refer to it – believes that it is true or valuable. But the important point is that it is shared widely.

We can and do also have language ideologies, and in the previous chapter, I tried to disabuse you of some of those ideologies (such as the ideology that there is a standard language that is better than other ways of speaking). So, ideologies are abstract ways of thinking about the world that almost always have real-world consequences in terms of behavior, including language. In their widest sense, ideologies are ways humans make sense of the world. How they work, circulate, spread, and so on is one area of research for the social sciences, and you may encounter other labels for similar phenomena, including **ontology**, **the imaginary**, and **discourses** (the latter of which should not be confused with discourses that are actual interactions).

So, gender is an ideological system. That is, we imagine a world in which there is masculinity and femininity and there are a whole host of kinds of people, institutions, and practices that get associated with those ideas. A simple example has to do with colors. In the US, the color blue is masculine and pink is feminine. These are strong associations for many people, with many men avoiding wearing pink except in certain circumstances in which the meaning of pink has been redefined (such as when professional American football players wear pink in support of breast cancer research – and even then, the pink is especially bright and 'aggressive' and 'masculine,' in my opinion). But the association is entirely arbitrary; if we all decided that pink meant masculine, then it would start meaning that. This is just a small and relatively harmless example, but there are others that are more serious, such as when people associate technical skill and expertise with masculinity. The point is that these are ideas that people have about the social categories of *masculinity/men/boys* and *femininity/women/ girls*.[1] They are not 'mere' ideas; they profoundly shape the lives and experiences of most humans. At the same time, gender ideologies and systems are far from immutable and shift throughout history.

So, *gender* (in the sense of the different practices, rules, institutions, customs, etc. of society built around sex difference) is not determined by *sex* (biology or hormones). The distinction between gender and sex is made often, but phrasing it this way makes it sound like the difference is clear, whereas the relationship between biology and gender is not straightforward. They are not unconnected to be sure, but the short version of reality is that there are very few ways in which biology definitively can *determine* a gender (as shown by the difficulties that sports bodies such as the International Olympic Committee [IOC] have in creating clear definitions of competition categories for men and women; see Aschwanden 2016b for an good explanation of the IOC's troubles). Even *sex* (the 'biological' category) is not as categorically binary as you may believe. Fausto-Sterling (2012) shows that there are many ways in which humans are born with combinations of chromosomes, genitals, and other biological traits which makes putting them into one of the two usual **sex categories** (**male** and **female**) impossible. You might think such births are extremely uncommon but the best estimate by Fausto-Sterling and colleagues (Blackless et al. 2000) is that such births occur between 1 in every 1,500 and 2,000 births. That means you probably know more than a few people born this way. The point is that even when it comes to something that we think of as immutable, we find that the body and mind are more closely connected than Cartesian dualism would have us think, and fetal and childhood experience can have a huge impact on development, even on supposed biological things like hormone release and the size of brain structures (for example, see Vythilingam et al. 2002). Moreover, as is true with almost every difference that is ever found for sex or gender, there is so much variability within sexes/genders that the differences between sexes/genders are significant only because you are comparing half the population with another half of the population (with large numbers, even small differences appear to be statistically significant, even if they're not really practically significant).[2]

So what is the relationship between sex and gender? The answer, as we will find over and over again, is that simplistic answers and categorization are not the stuff of the 'real world.' That is, hard and fast categories and linear reasoning are imposed on phenomena by human minds and cultures because the world is otherwise much too complicated for us to handle. We separate sex and gender so that we have **heuristics** for talking about the world. For example, we can talk about **sex** to refer to more biological things and **gender** to refer to social and ideological things. But as we've seen, the separation is not so easy, because the separation of the social and the biological is in fact itself an ideological way of looking at the world. So you can see why I long ago gave up trying to tease apart such large categorical distinctions and use gender for everything except sex acts, sexual desire, and sexual identity (which does not mean I am saying these are biological categories; they are just as ideologically organized).

So how do we understand **gender**? How do we 'know it when we see it?' The progress of thinking in this area has gone from thinking that gender *emerges* from biology, then to the idea that it is *built on* biology, then a view that it has nothing at all to do with biology, and finally to an understanding that gender is in tension with biology. This latest understanding is what is often called a **dialectical** relationship, because the two things are in tension, affect one another, and in the end create something in combination that is completely different from just adding the two together. (Yes, another story of making things more and more complex.) So, in the 1980s, theorists started to realize that gender was not inherent in a person, as mentioned above, but is about what someone *does*. In fact, one of the most well-known gender works at the time was by Candace West and Don Zimmerman (1987), called *Doing Gender*. In this view, we understand gender to be ways we do things differently depending on whether we think of ourselves as women or men. For language, that might mean that we tend to 'do' different things with our talk if we are a feminine or masculine person. For example, men might be more likely to use language to instruct than women.

A few years after the 'doing gender' approach became common, Judith Butler (1990) argued, in a sense, that gender has nothing to do with biology. Rather, it was all about **performativity** (revising an argument earlier proposed by Suzanne Kessler and Wendy McKenna [1978], among others). This idea of performativity will be important throughout the book, so let's explore it. Butler was not necessarily arguing that gender is a **performance** in the sense of a stage performance (but that was part of the idea). The argument is that by doing certain things and speaking, dressing, and so on, in particular ways, we are 'bringing into being' our gender, because other people recognize those actions as 'counting as' doing that gender. This comes from the idea of performativity in **speech act theory** of linguistics and philosophy as articulated by John Austin and John Searle (Austin 1962; Searle 1969). For example, once the right person says you are married, then you are married (who that person is depends on where you live and possibly your religion). So the ceremony (and especially the uttering of words in it) *creates* the marriage – there's no immediate physical change in the physical world, but the social world has changed. Of course, people need to recognize that these ceremonies 'count as' a wedding. So you're not married when you rehearse the wedding, even if it's all the same words in the same place, because the conditions aren't right and the right people aren't recognizing it (most importantly, the official of the court who gives the final certificate of marriage, at least in the US). Similarly, we do things that are recognized and 'count as' gender. To take the color example used previously, wearing (the right kind of) pink is recognized and counts as doing something feminine; in the case of the American football players, though, the pink they are wearing doesn't count as making them feminine. Gender is therefore a system of signals that count as femininity and masculinity, and anyone and anything can be masculine or feminine if they use the right performative formulas.

The backlash to this thinking is that it seems then that gender is not 'real,' that we could just as easily change gender as we could change our clothes. This is true to some extent, but that's not really how it works. In fact, Butler's book immediately after the one introducing her ideas was called *Bodies That Matter* (1993). We can see that bodies matter in that the gender system that is created for performativity has effects on people and their bodies – we can't *really* change our gender as easily as our clothes. But if you act in masculine ways enough, your body starts to get used to that groove and it gets harder and harder to change. If you transgress the right combination of performative practices (especially those that aren't ideologically aligned with your genital configuration), you are likely to have huge real-life bodily consequences. Think about it this way: Money is also basically a system of imaginary stuff, but it rules most of our physical environment, what we do, and where we go. So just because something is an abstract system doesn't mean it has no physical consequence. Gender is similar (as are many of human social systems) – we use ideologies to recognize and sort people into abstract categories, but this categorization system also organizes the institutions and ways of being that are the very building blocks of our lives.

So that's pretty much where we are with gender theory now. We're pulling apart the significance of thinking about gender as performative but bodily significant, and the ways in which these performative ideologies work. This view means that people are more often thinking to what extent their labeled bodies match their experienced or felt genders – their **gender identity**, and the ways they express their gender – their **gender expression**.[3] Such differentials are addressed in multiple ways depending on the person and the details of their gender identity. There is myriad variety in the ways that bodies that are assigned genders at birth can mismatch the gender a person feels (remember that not all bodies are clearly male or female at birth in first place). Some people will simply play with the symbols and practices of gender, some will adopt the manners and dress and other symbols of the opposite of their assignment, and some will adjust their bodies to line up better with their gender identity. But some such people are challenging the binary view of gender altogether and resist the categories themselves. The terms adopted by such people vary, but **non-binary** and **genderqueer** are two. In general, this variety of identity is often discussed under the umbrella term **Trans** (while people for whom gender identity is aligned with the gender assigned at birth are referred to as **cisgender** or simply cis, which is based on the Latin word meaning 'on this side of,' the opposite of the Latin *trans* 'across from').[4] Such labels are often contentious in this community, especially because for this group of people labels are much more than 'just labels'; they affect people who describe themselves as Trans in significant ways. For example, Trans people experience discrimination and violence at extremely high rates. The notion that gender is performative and is in tension with bodily feeling, activities, and form underlies much of the theorizing and understanding of Trans studies.

Throughout the book, I'll take this view of gender as performative and constructed, and we'll see how communities and cultures end up arguing about or coming to consensus about different forms of language and how they signify – or, more precisely, **index** – gender (we'll explore the idea of indexicality in the next couple of chapters).

Feminist theory, politics, and societal power

The study of gender is connected to the social movement most widely known as feminism, and feminism is still an important component of language and gender. In fact, one could easily argue that the field of language and gender (and the later incorporation of sexuality) exists because of feminism, and has been shaped by it, as we'll see in Chapter 5. Feminism starts with the observation that the binary way that humans are categorized in most societies – and certainly the ones in which feminism originated – creates asymmetries that provide one part of the binary (masculine) with more power, privilege, and freedom than another (feminine). In the earliest times in European-based societies (and to this day in others), women were not even granted full rights as humans, being denied the right, for example, to own property or participate politically. The 'first wave' of feminism was focused on securing **suffrage** – the right of women to vote, which in the US was achieved for all states by constitutional amendment in 1920 (it's only been about 100 years!). Why was it so hard for women to gain the vote? In short, women were not seen as people, but more like children.

As Mary Wollstonecraft put it in 1792, arguing that wom‹ have access to education: "women are not allowed to have strength of mind to acquire what deserves the name of virtue."

In the US and many other countries, once women won the vote, full equality was far from attained, as discrimination by gender was still legal and, in many cases, expected. Women were still treated by society in general as less than capable, and in the US, it is not until the 'second wave' of feminism that issues such as equal access to the workplace became a focus of activism. It's in this second wave that much of the study of language and gender began, as I discuss in Chapter 5. Linguists such as Robin Lakoff (1975) wondered to what extent the language used by and about women supported the inequalities that feminism was uncovering and fighting. As the feminist movement matured, it fractured considerably. I don't have space to go into the details here, but one can and could find more radical feminists for whom, to simplify a bit, heterosexual sex is always rape, but, at the same time, one can also find feminists who play down the power differentials while focusing on the differences between binary genders (to choose two mostly opposed 'types' of feminism).[5]

More changes in the political movement came about as a new generation discovered that there was still plenty of gender discrimination and gender-based power imbalance in the US and the world. Issues were (usually) less stark than, for example, the outright gender discrimination of the 1970s and 1980s. International awareness started to enter the US consciousness in issues such as female genital mutilation and human trafficking, and in the US, issues surrounding reproductive rights, sexual harassment, and sexual relations began to take center stage (and continue to this day in the recent #metoo movement). Issues of sex and power and control over reproduction are now the main issues that seem to concern feminist political activism, in addition to sexual minority and trans issues, which I discuss in the next section.

Gender, sexuality, and sexual identity and Queer linguistics

We've explored the complex set of categorization ideas and practices that make up *gender*, and some of the important ways that systems of power based on these categories are structured and are challenged.

Now, what about **sexuality**, a topic also promised in the book title? Let's start with the simple observation that, once we've decided on how we're going to talk about gender, the idea of sexuality has something to do with objects of **sexual desire**. When people talk about **sexual orientation**, they are usually talking about the gender category of the kind of person that someone desires in relation to the gender category the person desiring belongs to. So, if a man desires men, he is homosexual, while if he desires women, he's heterosexual. This way of thinking about things is probably familiar to you. It's also possible for someone to be **bisexual** and be attracted to both men and women, although this is often forgotten in ideological discussions of sexuality. All of these categories rely on the strict categorization of people into unproblematic groups of *men* and *women*, but when we start realizing that people's gender experiences are much more varied, we realize that something as simple as sexual orientation becomes complicated, as people may not feel much sexual desire at all (**asexuality**) or be attracted to any combination of gender (and other) identities (**pansexuality**).

Desire and sexual activity can be very private (and can be stigmatized), to the point that a sexual orientation may not be the same thing as a **sexual identity**. The distinction between these two types of categories of sexuality is essentially what gives rise to terms such as 'the closet,' in which someone who has a particular sexual orientation does not manifest it as a sexual identity (in which case, the sexual orientation is in the closet). So, for example, there are men who desire other men (sexual orientation) but do not have other behaviors that mark them as 'gay' (and this can work the other way around). This difference is important, especially when we get to ideas about language that identify someone's sexual identity – such kinds of speech do not identify sexual behavior, but rather sexual identity, which is a social category like gender.

Intersectionalities

My discussion so far in some ways mirrors the ways American and European feminists discussed gender until fairly recently – with women and men as the broad classes of people with similar interests, life experiences, and so on. But that's a big set of generalizations to make of over half the population of people on this earth, now busting through 7 billion in total. So when feminism began to speak 'for women,' the fact that it was mostly White middle-class heterosexual cisgendered women was problematic. Criticism sprang up early, as women of color wondered, for example, who would be hired to do the child care that the middle-class women were forgoing to join the paid workforce. In 1989, Kimberlé Crenshaw (1989) brought the term **intersectionality** into the feminist discourse by analyzing how Black women's employment experiences were qualitatively different than other people's. The term really took off with Crenshaw's (1991) article that showed how Black women experienced domestic violence and rape qualitatively differently than White women. That is, the Black women's experiences were not simply ones in which gender discrimination and racial discrimination were separate and additive, but interacted with each other to compound the discrimination in unique and pernicious ways. To draw on a cliché, it was more than the sum of the individual discriminations.

One of the most important contributions of this approach is to point out (or affirm) the idea that individual 'subjective' experiences are as important as, if not more important than, abstract 'objective' categories in feminist theory and activism (referred to more generally as **standpoint theory**), and in fact that such 'subjective' views allow us to understand the world in a more *objective* way since we have so many perspectives. In fact, such a view suggests that a true and complete objective understanding of the social world is not possible, because there is 'no view from nowhere.' So rather than simply fragmenting the categories of gender (and other social constructs such as race, ethnicity, and class), intersectionality provides a way of understanding how gender and other social constructs actually affect the lives of people who identify with, and are identified with, those categories.

Challenging gender binaries

Of course, all of these intersectionalities rely on ideologies created by social processes around us and in which we participate, and that may or may not be shared. So, one of the notions about gender in European-based societies and certainly in the American one that I am part of is the idea that gender is 'fluid.' In light of that fact, I've been lately trying to refer not so much to 'women' and 'men,' but to 'feminine people' and 'masculine people.' I like this system because it does not remove gender but points out that it is a modifier and not an essence. Moreover, it reminds us that we are all *people*, which is a small measure of keeping the shared humanity at the same time as acknowledging different experiences and feelings.

As I've discussed throughout this chapter, one of the big challenges that has been with gender theory and feminist theory for a long time is how do we still talk about gender when there is a fragmenting of gender, both as the binary system and as a way of analyzing experience across other sorts of identity categories. This is a huge question that many brilliant people have wrestled with and it comes down to acknowledging the vast complexity and nuance of the world as it runs up against our human need to understand larger patterns of human relationships, and most importantly, to change the world so that it is more peaceful and equitable. I suggest that the answer to this huge question is exactly in the tension between the messiness of actual lived experience and life stories (or just stories and conversations) that people have and their struggle to understand *why* things happen to them and what motivates them to do what they do. That is, experience is particular, but it is influenced by a host of widespread and powerful forces, some of which are changeable. In the main chapters of this book, we'll see how language fits into this view of gender, since language is something that we experience in particular through stories and conversations, but, at the same time, it is a shared resource that is unevenly accessible to people. We'll also see, however, that language is implicated in gender in important ways. In the next chapter, I present a short overview of the field of language and gender to contextualize these ideas.

Notes

1 Why not just say *masculinity* and *femininity*? This comes from my view that, in fact, the '-*inities*' aren't somehow derivative of the other categories, even though they are related, as seen by the fact that there are 'masculine women.'

2 See a great post on this statistical problem by Christie Aschwanden about nutrition studies, although the principles are still the same (Aschwanden 2016a).

3 The fact that identity and expression are treated with separate terms, even in relatively popular contexts, shows the wide influence of Butler's work in convincing the world that expression and identity are separate.
4 See Chapter 1 for an explanation of capitalization of named groups.
5 For example, see https://witchwind.wordpress.com/2013/12/15/piv-is-always-rape-ok.

References

Aschwanden, C. (2016a). You can't trust what you read about nutrition. http://fivethirtyeight.com/features/you-cant-trust-what-you-read-about-nutrition/. Accessed June 20, 2018.

Aschwanden, C. (2016b). The Olympics are still struggling to define gender. https://fivethirtyeight.com/features/the-olympics-are-still-struggling-to-define-gender. Accessed June 20, 2018.

Austin, J. (1962). *How to Do Things with Words*. Harvard University Press, Cambridge, MA.

Baker, P. (2008). *Sexed Texts: Language, Gender and Sexuality*. Equinox Publishing, Oakville, CT.

Blackless, M., Charuvastra, A., Derryck, A., Fausto-Sterling, A., Lauzanne, K., and Lee, E. (2000). How Sexually Dimorphic Are We? Review and Synthesis. *American Journal of Human Biology*, 12(2):151–166.

Butler, J. (1990). *Gender Trouble: Feminism and the Subversion of Identity*. Routledge, New York, NY.

Butler, J. (1993). *Bodies that Matter: On the Discursive Limits of "Sex."* Routledge, New York, NY.

Crenshaw, K. (1989). Demarginalizing the Intersection of Race and Sex: A Black Feminist Critique of Antidiscrimination Doctrine, Feminist Theory, and Antiracist Politics. *University of Chicago Legal Forum*, 1989(1):139–167.

Crenshaw, K. (1991). Mapping the Margins: Intersectionality, Identity Politics, and Violence Against Women of Color. *Stanford Law Review*, 43(6):1241–1299.

Fausto-Sterling, A. (2012). *Sex/Gender: Biology in a Social World*. Routledge, New York, NY.

Kessler, S. J. and McKenna, W. (1978). *Gender: An Ethnomethodological Approach*. University of Chicago Press, Chicago, IL.

Lakoff, R. T. (1975). *Language and Woman's Place*. Harper & Row, New York.

Money, J. (1955). Hermaphroditism, Gender and Precocity in Hyperadrenocorticism: Psychologic Findings. *Bulletin of the Johns Hopkins Hospital*, 96:253–264.

Rubin, G. (1975). The Traffic in Women: Notes on the "Political Economy" of Sex. In Reiter, R. R., editor, *Toward an Anthropology of Women*, pages 157–210. Monthly Review Press, New York, NY.

Searle, J. R. (1969). *Speech Acts: An Essay in the Philosophy of Language.* Cambridge University Press, New York, NY.

Vythilingam, M., Heim, C., Newport, J., Miller, A. H., Anderson, E., Bronen, R., Brummer, M., Staib, L., Vermetten, E., Charney, D. S., Nemeroff, C. B., and Bremner, J. D. (2002). Childhood Trauma Associated with Smaller Hippocampal Volume in Women with Major Depression. *American Journal of Psychiatry*, 159(12):2072–2080.

West, C. and Zimmerman, D. H. (1987). Doing Gender. *Gender & Society*, 1(2):125–151.

Wollstonecraft, M. (1792). *A Vindication of the Rights of Woman*. James Moore, Dublin.

Chapter 4

How we got here

A brief history of the study of language, gender, and sexuality

Noticing that gender is in language and that how a person speaks is related to their gender identity is not new. Linguists (and no doubt others) have long noted situations in which gender is related to language. For example, in 1958, John Fischer published a study of school children and how they pronounce words ending in -*ing* in English: for example, *working* or *workin'* (in the International Phonetic Alphabet [IPA] of my pronunciation, [wɚkɪŋ] vs. [wɚkɪn]). This early study only had a few participants but found a difference in the rates of the boys' and girls' use of the alternation, with the girls using more -*ing* than the boys. Interestingly, the biggest difference found was between a boy he identified as a "model boy" and the other "typical boys," with the typical boys using more of the -*in* variant. So, by 1958, linguists had already started to perform studies on how gender affects language use.

Even earlier, linguists had also found a few cultures in which different 'rules for speaking' were expected depending on gender, among other social categories relevant in each culture. An early example of this was a study of the **Koasati** people by Mary Haas in 1944.[1] Koasati is a Native American Language spoken by approximately 200 people in Louisiana, USA (although when Haas was working there were no doubt many more speakers). Haas reported that for certain morphemes, men use a different pronunciation than women. Haas documented six different sets of rules for this difference, but the majority involve a change of consonants to [s] or an addition of [s]. Haas went on to mention that these differences are well known to the speakers, to the point that they are used in telling stories even when the gender of the speaker is not the same as that of the character (that is, if a man tells a story and a he quotes a woman, he uses the 'women's language'). Haas's short discussion of other languages with similar gender differences shows that the use of lexical and pronunciation differences to signal gender of speaker is a widespread feature of human language, even if it is usually not as categorical as in Koasati.

Lakoff's insights

While the studies of gender and language just discussed had been around for some time, the beginning of language and gender as a subfield in linguistics is usually traced to the publication of Robin Lakoff's (1973) article and her expansion of that article into a short book (1975) called *Language and Woman's Place*. Lakoff was channeling the second-wave feminist zeitgeist of the late 1960s and early 1970s in which women were discovering the myriad ways that society was organized to advantage men; a social organization of institutions, traditions, laws, ideologies, and practices often referred to as a single entity: 'the **patriarchy**.'[2] The second wave of feminism is characterized most clearly by the uncovering of women's lives and accomplishments that had been invisible before, and the emergence of women into fields of work that had previously been open only to men. Even then, this movement was a struggle: A lawyer who came of age in the 1960s tells me of her first appearance before a male judge in the 1970s in which the judge had to be cajoled into accepting that she could 'handle' the stresses of the courtroom.

In the US at that time, there were a lot of ways in which women were disadvantaged, sometimes blatantly but often subtly. One such subtle way is through **hegemony**, as articulated by the Italian Marxist philosopher Antonio Gramsci (1971). The working of hegemonic power is different from power that operates with, for example, brute physical force or economic subjugation. Hegemonic power works through ideas and ideologies, so that the powerless believe in the system that causes their powerlessness, and often even collude in its perpetuation. So, a goal of second wave feminism was to explore and expose the ideologies and processes through which this hegemony works. Accordingly, one of the activities of feminist groups was 'consciousness raising,' in which women were invited to groups to discuss ways in which the patriarchy was hegemonically organized so that women accepted their subordination and even participated in it, policing other women who did not fit into traditional categories (such as the lawyer mentioned above, who was disapproved of for working full time while having a family).

In the early 1970s, Robin Lakoff was a young linguist working on syntax, semantics, and pragmatics, and participating in the women's movement in Berkeley, California. She noticed that language was one of the ways in which patriarchy did its hegemonic work and set out to use the tools of linguistics to show this – in a sense, to do some 'linguistic consciousness raising.' She used introspection, the main method of generative linguistics, to think about how women were expected to speak differently from men and what that meant. She also proposed some ways that language creates a view of women that is discriminatory. She argued that the main effect of these differences is to "submerge a woman's personal identity," suggesting she is "not a serious person with individual views" (Lakoff 1975, p. 7). The effect, then, is that "women are systematically denied access to power." But, even if they use language that is more powerful, there is a problem: They are not 'ladies' and thus less successful women than if they used more powerless language. This is the **double bind** that Lakoff details further in the book. Lakoff breaks her argument into two threads: language used (or expected to be used) by women, and language used about women (note that these are essentially two of the three main parts of this book, interaction and categorization, respectively).

Lakoff suggested that the language which is expected to be used by women signals a number of powerless and unserious aspects of femininity. First, she argued that the domains in which women were expected to have more elaborated vocabulary suggest less serious and less worldly topics. In particular, she argued that women used more elaborate color terminology such as *sea foam* and *chartreuse* rather than simple terms such as *green*. This elaboration signals an expertise in domestic affairs such as fashion and decorating. She also suggested that women were more likely to use hedges such as *I think*, arguing that these forms reduce the strength of the assertion that speaker makes. Another suggestion was that women used more '**tag questions**' and rising intonation, which signaled a similar lack of certainty and power. A tag question is one added to the end of a sentence, and in many cases can be heard as asking for confirmation, as in *You were born in 1984, weren't you?* It's not hard to hear the uncertainty in many such examples, and Lakoff suggested that women use more of these and that it signaled such uncertainty. She made similar claims about the use of rising intonation on sentences that aren't questions, for example, in the answer that Stephanie gives in the following:

KIM: When was Scott born?
STEPHANIE: 1967?

Keep in mind that Lakoff is writing in the early 1970s, and since then, rising intonation has expanded in who uses it and how many people do (we'll discuss this more later in the book). But you can hear the uncertainty in the answer in the example above, and it is this uncertainty that Lakoff argued was more characteristic (and expected) of how American women spoke. Finally, she suggested that women are more polite for the same reason – **politeness** is a way of softening what you want (we discuss this in the next chapter). Through these forms, she argued that the expectation was that womanhood – and femininity more generally – was defined by its powerlessness and lack of individual agency.

Lakoff also argued that there was an inequality in the ways that English referred to women and men. First, she took on the term *lady*. She argued that women are referred to and addressed as *ladies* and not *women* because *lady* is a **euphemism** for *women*, and that euphemisms are used to discuss taboo things (for example, *powder room* or even *rest room* for *toilet*). Therefore, women (and not men) are something to be hidden – ladies are refined and pleasant, like an air freshener in the powder room. Moreover, *lady* is used as a modifier when it is socially expected that the referent is a man: *lady doctor* rather than just *doctor* referring to a doctor who is a woman. In such cases, she argued that the *lady* modifier not only indicates that the referent is a woman – but then why not *woman doctor*? – but the term also diminishes the feminine person in some way.

Lakoff also noted a few asymmetries in nouns, in which the masculine is **unmarked** and the feminine is **marked**.[3] Some of these term pairs have actually fallen out of use more recently, such as *waiter-waitress* (now *server*) and *stewardess-steward* (now usually *flight attendant*). The feminine forms are marked because they are longer, in some cases made longer through the use of a **diminutive**, forms that exist in languages to make the main lexical item smaller or less significant (another way that these forms create a view of women as less than full adult people).

You will probably already have guessed that the asymmetry that was most glaring for Lakoff was the system of formal titles for women and men: *Mr.*, *Miss*, and *Mrs.* In this asymmetry, men can only be one thing, a full-fledged 'mister,' but women are either a married 'missus' or a an unmarried 'miss.' The latter also has connotations of being a girl and not grown up. Either way, in the heterosexual logic of this system, a woman is addressed based on her status with respect to a man, while a man is always a man (remember that Lakoff was writing before the invention of *Ms.*).

Lakoff's work was limited by the fact that her observations were not the result of actually recording and analyzing men and women, and further that she was discussing only the language of an assumed White, middle-to-upper class, heterosexual, cisgendered woman. But her observations were theoretically important and, more important, even though she did not test them, they were testable.

The search for difference and dominance

To say that Lakoff's book was influential is an understatement. Because she made her claims from introspection, she opened a whole raft of research avenues as researchers attempted to confirm her claims or add nuance to them. They investigated all sorts of types of language to see if and how men and women used language differently, and if differences were found, whether these differences implicated power relationships between women and men. Many began simply by counting: do women use more or less of some way of speaking than men?

As researchers began recording conversations on tape, and transcribing them, they first stumbled across the issue of categorization.

In order to count something like a tag question, you need to know what a tag question is. That doesn't seem too hard, but often what seems to be a single form might have different communicative functions depending on exactly how it is used. Holmes (1984; see also Holmes 1995) noted two different kinds of tag questions, and for only one type – the **affective** – did women use more than men (this study is explained in more detail in Chapter 6). When Cameron et al. (1989) reproduced this study, they found a similar pattern but also had some difficulties with categorization. Importantly, in addition to gender, they categorized speakers as powerless or powerful, and powerless speakers used no affective tag questions. This result suggested that women didn't use more tag questions because they are powerless. The point of this example is not to get into the weeds of whether and how the generalization about tag questions is true. Rather, the point is that generalization such as 'women use more tag questions' is not as easy to verify as it seems, and as more studies were done on the claims in Lakoff, the more complex the answers became, and the less sweeping generalizations and explanations seemed to make sense. This was particularly true of explanations that relied (usually covertly) on women's (and men's, but usually women's) character, such as "women are more status conscious" or "women are powerless," and so on. However, it took a heated debate about just that to move beyond this view, which we'll get to after a short look at some other important issues in early language and gender research.

An aside about identity

You may have noticed that besides gender, the identities of speakers in these studies aren't identified. The standpoint taken is that these identities are unmarked, which means an assumption that they are White Anglo, relatively economically privileged, cisgendered, and heterosexual. This view is not an oversight on my part but reflects the focus of early work on language and gender (which to some extent continues to this day). This focus on the most privileged of women was common in early feminist work, and (as mentioned in the previous chapter) such work was criticized for its focus on, and universalizing of, women in this category.

Once again, this focus is part of the history and subsequent organization of the field, although you'll find that the next section discusses some work in other parts of the world. Nevertheless, there is little early work on the language, gender, and race and ethnicity. In 1989, Kimberlé Crenshaw suggested the notion of intersectionality, which stresses that Black women are subordinated by both categories, Black and Woman, and that the intersection leads to issues that are qualitatively different from 'adding them up.' It's worth keeping in mind while reading about these early studies that the focus on particular identities may have influenced the types of questions that were asked.

Other early work around the world

While Lakoff's work is the most cited work on language and gender in English from the 1970s onward, there was early work going on in non-English languages, although, in general, it started somewhat later than Lakoff. For example, from about the same period there was work on German (see Hellinger [1995] for a summary of early work on German). This culminated in a work that, like Lakoff's work, inspired feminist-focused scholarship on language and gender in German: *Deutsche als Mannersprache* (*German as a Man's Language*) by Luise Pusch (Pusch 1984). Pusch was a journalist who observed similar patterns as Lakoff but in German, and similarly argued that women and men had two different 'languages.' Senta Troemel-Ploetz (1982, 1984), working around the same time, made arguments about ways that men dominate the conversation, arguing that women are more often interrupted. While most of the patterns she described were not found in later studies, like Lakoff, her work inspired a number of studies in language and gender on German and is thus important.

On the other side of the world in Japan, there was a similar focus on the idea that a separate 'Japanese women's language' existed. However, gender differences for language are recorded from ancient times in Japan, and as Inoue (2002) argues, were used for the nationalization project in the early 20th century. But there was parallel work in the 1970s in Japan, as outlined by Yukawa and Saito (2004). Akiko Jugaku's (1979) book, roughly translated as *The Japanese Language and Women*, also made observations similar to Lakoff's. But as Yukawa and Saito note, Jugaku went further than Lakoff in highlighting the ideological forces that collectively create the marked category of woman. Specifically, they explain that Jugaku "theorized that the concept consists of three components: (1) language designed for a female audience, (2) topics chosen for a female audience, and (3) linguistic strategies used to display that the speaker is a woman" (Yukawa and Saito 2004, p. 66). Yukawa and Saito point out that while these topics resemble Lakoff's, they place more emphasis on the general ideological basis that affects the ideal way of speaking for women than on the ways that women speak in real life, as Lakoff did. One of the most interesting points that they make, however, is that even though Jugaku initially had an important impact on the field of language and gender in Japan, ideas about language and gender imported from the UK and the US eventually had more impact in Japan. They argue that there was a movement away from seeing women's language as an ideological construction and toward the description and even recreation of the idea of a separate women's language. This development prefigures some of the debates in language and gender in English-dominant work pitting 'difference' against 'dominance,' as we will see soon.

Gender patterns in language change

At the same time as Lakoff and Jukaku were making their claims about women's language and difference in grammar and interaction, linguists were discovering that there were statistical differences between genders in pronunciation and other forms in many languages, and that when language changes, men and women often participate in those changes at different rates. These patterns will be the subject of Chapter 7, but it's important to remember that this work was going on at the same time as Lakoff's and was part of what came next. Researchers working in the field known as **sociolinguistic variation and change** found that in general, women tended to use language that was relatively more 'standard' than men. (I put 'standard' in scare quotes because I don't like this term; it is a construction and idealization of language. That is, as discussed in Chapter 2, it's a social and ideological construct, and in fact there is variation in this 'standard' just as there is in all language.) So, there's a pattern in which women, for example, use more of the *-ing* variant than men, who use more of the *-in'* variant (see Eckert [1990] and Labov [1990]) for discussions and disagreements about this pattern, which we'll explore more fully in Chapter 7). Paradoxically, women generally tend to adopt new ways of speaking more than men (although it depends on the particular new way of speaking). It's paradoxical because such new forms are pretty much by definition *not* 'standard.' In general, before the late 1980s, the study of sociolinguistic variation often takes a view that women are inherently or biologically predisposed to speak in certain ways (an **essentialist** view). For example, it's claimed that women are linguistically insecure, women are more verbally skilled than men, and that women are more status conscious. Nevertheless, the patterns the variationists were finding were real, and suggested that the other research looking for gender differences in language use was valid and might yield real results.

Disputing the causes of differences

The next important phase of work on language and gender was not mainly a disagreement about whether there were differences of any kind, but what might cause those differences. Remember that Lakoff made claims not only about how women are referred to, but how women were expected to speak. These claims were taken to be claims about how women actually spoke, and it is these claims that led to a more general 'search for difference' between expectation and reality in the 1970s and 1980s. Examples would include studies about whether women use more tag questions than men, the meaning of statements with rising intonation and whether women use them more, and whether women are more verbally polite than men. We'll get to the mixed and somewhat complex findings of these studies later in the book (see Chapter 6). In general, though – at least in the 1980s – there was a consensus in linguistics that some gender differences existed (especially in terms of turn-taking and politeness).

While linguists disputed how well these patterns held up, in general, the idea that there were some global differences between men and women (usually assumed to be White, cisgendered, and middle class) was rarely criticized. And as Cameron (1998) points out, these differences were often generalized over different subgroups of men and women, as well as within different speech situations and institutional contexts. The heat of the academic exchange about this research was generated in the competing explanations about the global gender differences.

In 1982, Daniel Maltz and Ruth Borker published an article in which they proposed that the differences in the ways that women and men talk are analogous to the differences found across cultures. In other words, cultures learn that different ways of speaking are, for example, polite or impolite. So, it's claimed that North American English-speaking cultures are more direct than Greek-speaking cultures (see, for example, Tannen 1981). In the context of gender, it was argued that boys and girls tend to grow up playing with same-sex groups, and thus learn different ways of interacting in those different groups. When they interact as adults, there is miscommunication because, for example, men who interrupt are used to being interrupted themselves by other men, and from their perspective, women are simply not being 'competitive' enough in their **conversational styles**.

Maltz and Borker's approach to explaining gender differences in conversation is often referred to as the **difference** approach or the **cultural difference** approach. The other perspective is referred to as the **dominance** approach, sometimes also called the **deficit** approach (although the latter is actually slightly different). The dominance approach focuses on the power dynamics between men and women. So, taking the above example, it is not that overlapping or interrupting has a different 'meaning' or elicits a different response in conversations between women as opposed to men, but rather that men *treat women differently* in conversations, interrupting them more often in order to dominate conversations. This explanation for differences has a number of different variants, such as the idea that women are ideologically expected to be more polite in a culture (see Lakoff's observations mentioned earlier), and therefore are less likely to interrupt, whereas men don't have the same expectations for politeness. This version of the dominance/deficit perspective removes some agency from men's behavior, so that men are not seen as actively dominating women, but are rather 'being men' (which, however, entails displaying power and dominating women).

The debate between these two perspectives, which were really not quite as disparate as some of the heat of the argument would have one believe, culminated in the publication of Deborah Tannen's *You Just Don't Understand: Women and Men in Conversation* (Tannen 1990), which explained the difference approach to non-linguists. The book was insanely popular, spending nearly four years on the *New York Times* bestseller list. Although Tannen does talk about men's structural power in American society, most of the criticisms of her explanation of the difference approach took her to task for not being political enough, and for not calling men to account for the effects of dominating moves in conversation. Some criticisms were criticism of the difference approach itself for not engaging with issues of power, but many were quite emotional and *ad hominem*. In fact, much energy was spent on criticizing the difference approach, mainly because it suggests (as much cross-cultural communication also does) that power differences don't play as much of a role in conversational styles as the dominance approach suggests (although, once again, there is a clear implication that men tend to focus on power and dominance, both over other men and over women).

The debate lost steam after most researchers realized that the argument was not really an empirical one but a personal and political one. Cameron's (1998) critiques of both the difference and dominance camps are instructive, even as her article was published in the waning days of the debate. Cameron points out both methodological and theoretical issues with both approaches. The criticism of the dominance approach is one that just because men and women use different linguistic strategies and forms at different rates doesn't mean that the men are dominating; the researchers in these cases are deciding ahead of time what the meanings of the purported differences are. But Tannen's (and Maltz and Borker's and others') research shows that linguistic forms and especially discourse strategies can have variable and sometimes opposite social meanings, so deciding ahead of time that a way of speaking is powerless is problematic. It is also easy to fall into the trap of finding what you think you will find in linguistic data; if you imagine that a woman is powerless in a conversation, you'll probably find some evidence for it. (Before you get too excited about that statement, be clear that I'm not saying, nor were difference researchers, that there aren't power differences, just that one needs to be careful in demonstrating them!) The critique of the difference approach has to do with the downplaying of overall social power, but moreover the observation that the same strategies are treated differently when employed by men and women, that in a sense men have more power to define the strategies than women (and that 'women's strategies' often end up as being seen as powerless because of their association with women, not the other way around). To repeat a refrain you will read often in this book, things are a lot more complicated than either difference or dominance.

Communities of practice

So, how to address the complexity in a way that doesn't give up the project of finding out how gender affects language use? After the difference/dominance debate, the field moved away from the idea of gender as an all-encompassing identity in which all men and all women are lumped together, and moved toward a more nuanced view that looked at how being a feminine or masculine person was significant in interactions in smaller communities and groups. The idea is not that gender is remade or irrelevant in different speaking situations or events, but that gender is relevant in different ways in these more particular situations. In order to do this, language and gender theorists needed a way to keep an eye on both the norms of the smaller social organization and the wider effects of gender. In the words of the title of the article that introduced these ideas (Eckert and McConnell-Ginet 1992), they needed to "think practically and look locally." Penny Eckert and Sally McConnell-Ginet were also explicitly trying to integrate the notions of difference and dominance to suggest that theoretically, we should figure out how difference leads to dominance in some situations and not in others. They note that (1992, p. 462):

> we have organized much of our discussion around difference on the one hand (especially as a component of gender identities) and power on the other (especially male dominance as a component of gender relations). However, we have tried to shift attention away from an opposition of the two and toward the processes through which each feeds the other to produce the concrete complexities of

language as used by real people engaged in social practice. .... Not only are difference and dominance both involved in gender, but they are also jointly constructed and prove ultimately inseparable.

Eckert and McConnell-Ginet go on to ask what it means to be, for example, a man in a college fraternity as opposed to a man in a book club with friends, as opposed to what it means to be a woman in those two contexts. These smaller communities are called **communities of practice**: Groups of people who come together around some activity. Eckert and McConnell-Ginet's approach is appealing in that it brings **agency** into the theoretical discussion. In other words, this approach conceives of speakers not simply as doing something just because of their gender, but as doing something because it is a valuable move to make in their community at that particular moment, taking their gender/sexual identity into account. Larger patterns easily appear as people make similar choices about what to say and how to say it in all of these different communities (as I, for example, move from the class-room to the faculty meeting and then dinner with my family).

Performativity and indexing gender

Two years before Eckert and McConnell-Ginet published their work on communities of practice, Judith Butler, a philosopher, published *Gender Trouble* (Butler 1990), a work that popularized the idea that gender is performative, as discussed in Chapter 3. As a reminder, the notion that gender is performative does not mean that we always put on a costume and are never our 'real' selves. Rather, the notion of performativity comes from speech act theory, in the sense that we need to be able to read meanings from repeated actions and symbols. That is, there are certain actions that conventionally 'count' as femininity or masculinity. So gender in some ways becomes a problem of conventionalization.

In this view, linguistic forms that are connected to genders are not due to some inherent qualities of being a man or woman (for example, 'toughness' or 'politeness'). Rather, they are conventionally connected to those groups through ideologies about gender. Note that this view is compatible with the idea of communities of practice, in which the meanings of actions are negotiated within each group. In the view of performativity, each action or linguistic form has a meaning based on the history and norms of that group, and those meanings can also be renegotiated and changed. In other words, when a person says something in a particular way, other people in that community interpret it in terms of a framework they understand and can add meaning to. One important aspect is that these acts are repeated so that they become connected to their contexts of use (or the 'kind of' person doing them, within some system of categorization).

The view of performativity eventually had a profound effect on language and gender theory because it meant that theorists could argue that different ways of speaking that pattern by gender are not due to an inherent or even learned psychological trait of women (or men, but it was usually women). Rather, these differences are part of the cultural project of categorizing people by gender, which the speaker participates in. Linguistic forms that pattern by gender therefore recreate the categories themselves. This perspective is truly about the difference gender makes rather than simply gender difference.

But why do some forms get an attached gender, and what does it mean for a linguistic form to 'be connected' to a kind of person (that is, a gender)? Linguists talk about meaning in different ways, depending on how the linguistic form gets related to its meaning. If the relation process is completely arbitrary, as it is for most words, then we call that meaning process **symbolic**. For example, the word-form *tree* is not related to any essence of being a tree. On the other hand, the word *buzz* has at least a partial **iconic** relationship to its meaning, since the sound resembles the sound in the word meaning (if you imitate a bee flying around, you will probably make the sound [z]).

The meaning process we are really interested in here, though, is one in which the linguistic form says something about the context of use, such as the identity of the speaker. This meaning process is called **index-icality**. Here, the meaning has to do with **context**, and in linguistics this is usually the context of speaking. You no doubt use different ways of speaking to your friends than you do with, for example, work colleagues or family. This change is something you or your friends notice, and if you switch your way of speaking in the wrong context, people will notice. This is true not just of who you are addressing and the 'formality' of the context; it is also true of the speaker – we learn things about the identity of the speaker by what kind of language they use.

You might be already anticipating that indexicality fits into performativity, because performativity is really a kind of indexical meaning: Performativity is meaning that is read from repeated actions – those actions become indexed to the gender of the person performing them. So in language and gender, performativity and indexicality are tightly tied together. In the early 1990s, there were developments in how language and gender theory approached indexicality. One way of thinking about this relationship is that any linguistic form that patterns with gender simply indexes a particular gender.

This performative connection between gender and linguistic form makes sense; some linguistic forms, especially pitch, most often work this way (women's voices are statistically higher in pitch). But Elinor Ochs (1992) suggests (in a way that is also consistent with the theory of performativity) that sometimes gender is indexed indirectly. **Indirect indexicality** is a concept that describes how some indexical meanings get connected to gender categories. The process works through ideologies about what kinds of traits constitute gender (and the fact that there are categories in the first place). For example, women might be seen as more refined than men, and men rougher and coarser than women. In fact, these are the stereotypical traits that Ochs uses from Japanese society to make her argument about indexing gender. Ochs argues that being 'refined' or 'coarse' are stances that are associated with femininity and masculinity, respectively. Those stances are directly indexed in Japanese by certain sentence final particles, small words that Japanese has at the end of sentences. *Wa* indexes a refined stance and *zo* and *ze* index a coarse stance. The sentence final particles are indexed to gender not directly in the sense that using *ze* directly marks someone as a man, but it indirectly indexes masculinity because one of the ways (a certain kind of) masculinity is created is by taking a coarse stance. Figure 4.1 shows this in graphical form. In this figure, acts refer to speech acts such as *compliments* and *requests*, while activities refer to more extended speaking activities and genres such as *lecturing*, *gossiping*, and *explaining* (you may even be able to suggest how those acts and activities might be gendered in your culture, if similar speech forms exist).

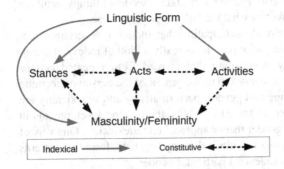

So a lot of the theorizing on language and gender in the last few decades has been related to exploring how these patterns of indirect indexicality and performativity work. Questions arise such as: How are gender ideologies structured so that stances, acts, and activities can fit into them? How do language forms work to index different stances, acts, and activities? Why do such stances, acts, and activities get connected to different genres? We will touch on all of these questions as the book unfolds, and see that the picture becomes pretty complicated, far beyond the neat lines in the general schematic in Figure 4.1.

Some of the work on ideologies has to do with what is called **language ideologies**, which I'll mention here since it is a theoretical approach that affects language and gender studies and began to flourish about the same time as the notion of indexing gender. (It's heavy with terminology, too, so get ready for definitions.) This research focuses on how people think about language and how language fits into the social world. For example, the idea that there is one correct way to speak that is better than other ways of speaking is a language ideology, as is what exactly that 'better way of speaking' sounds like. These ideas intersect with language, gender, and sexuality because people have ideologies about how language 'reflects' these social categories. Irvine and Gal (2000) articulate a framework with which to discuss these ideologies and how they work. They propose three main processes in which "linguistic features are seen as reflecting and expressing broader cultural images of people and activities" (2000, p. 37). **Iconization** takes a linguistic form that is connected to a social group and assumes that the connection is related to "a social group's inherent nature or essence" (2000, p. 37). In terms of gender, one can imagine a masculine or feminine trait being iconically imbued in the language used by men or women (as in the Japanese sentence final particles mentioned above). **Fractal recursivity** describes a situation where an opposition such as masculinity and femininity gets replayed at different levels of social organization. So, for example, we might find that the opposition between femininity and masculinity (and some quality of that relationship) becomes relevant within a conversation even among speakers of the same gender, perhaps recreating power asymmetries. Finally, **erasure** "renders some persons or activities (or sociolinguistic phenomena) invisible" (2000, p. 38). This could be the idea that men and women speak with different languages, assuming men and women are homogeneous, or even that men don't have a distinctive way of speaking while women do. It's useful to use these processes to understand how gender/sexual identity works, and has been a useful theoretical advance for understanding, for example, how difference can relate to and be part of dominance relations in language and gender, because it shows how everyday uses can reflect larger patterns and beliefs about both gender and language.

Some final theoretical machinery helps us to further specify how identity gets created and performed in interactions. Introduced by Kira Hall and Mary Bucholz, this framework is called **tactics of intersubjectivity** (Bucholtz and Hall 2004). They suggest three dimensions of tactics that people use. The first is a dimension of similarity versus difference, the poles of which they call **adequation** and **distinction**. The idea is that in interaction, people do things to show similarity and difference with other people (present or not) and thus create categories with those people. A second tactic is along the dimensions of **authentication** and **denaturalization**, in which interaction and language are used to authenticate an identity as someone's 'natural' identity, or to mark a performative gender action as somehow not authentic (to 'denaturalize' it). Finally, there is **authorization** and **illegitimation**, which refer to the ways societies, cultures, and institutions allow certain categories of identity, and allow certain people into those categories. For gender/ sexuality, certain relationships are authorized, for example, by the government: in many countries, a woman can have a husband but saying she has a wife is unintelligible, and thus illegitimate (we will see this at work in the next chapter). All of these tactics can be used at different times (and in different ways with respect to language) to reinforce gender categories and connect individuals to these categories.

Bringing in sexual identity and desire

Bucholtz and Hall's work discussed at the end of the last section came about because they were in a new debate in language, gender, and sexuality: They were writing in response to a criticism by Kulick (2000) of some of their work, and of what is sometimes called 'queer linguistics' more generally. That criticism argued that queer linguistics is overly concerned with the social categorizations of sexual identity and less about the actual desires underlying those sexual categories. To understand why there was a dispute in the first place, let's back up a bit to see that this theoretical disagreement follows a history of studying sexual identities and desires in language. Cameron and Kulick (2003) provide a detailed history of this study, starting in the early 20th century (see, for example, Legman 1941). In general, there's a move from language used by closeted gay men early on, to the notion that there is a 'gay style' that gay men used. There were some studies in the 1990s that focused on trying to describe linguistic features of this style, or at least the features that people recognized, with similar descriptions for lesbian styles (see, for example, Gaudio 1994, Leap 1996, Moonwomon 1997).

The critique of work on language and sexual identity is in some part a reaction to the uptake of Butlerian performance theory in this area, in which researchers were showing that linguistic forms were transportable to different identities and available to be used in creative ways that were 'detachable' from the identities with which they were originally indexed. An example par excellence of language being used performatively for identity work in this way is Kira Hall's (1995) analysis of language used by workers who answered 'fantasy lines': telephone lines in which people called (and paid) to have people of different (purported) identities talk to them in sexual ways. Hall shows how speakers use language to create these identities, including some workers who create identities very different from their 'authentic identities' (for example, a White man who creates a Black woman persona). Another example is Barret's (1999) analysis of drag queens, who use language not only performatively but also in performance, and who create not simply a category of woman but specifically of a 'drag queen,' using specific linguistic forms (like a high-pitched voice) to connect to very recognizable forms of femininity. These studies bring into sharp relief the constructed and performative approach to language and gender/sexuality, so that it is easy to imagine that linguistic forms are something that people can take out of their 'linguistic closet' and put on at will. The critique which returns to desire is based on the observation that people can't really change these categories as easily as they can change their clothes. Rather, they are more deeply felt identities and identifications, categories that people want to be a part of (or categories that people don't want to be a part of) and use language to help fulfill these desires.

Emerging trends: Translinguistics, embodiment, and affect

This observation and critique prefigures recent work in the relatively merged field of language, gender, and sexuality, in which desires and feelings begin to be reincorporated into theory without losing sight of how language is part of the performativity of the ideological categories that cultures build around language and sexuality (that is, cultural conceptions of what it means to be a man or a woman). These trends can be seen in wider theorizing around gender and sexuality, but are increasingly important in the language and gender/sexuality subfield. One way this is seen is in the study of the language of Trans identities and other identities that challenge the fixity and binarity of gender ideologies, and even the fixity of the distinction between the biological/body and the performativity of gender. Questions are being raised about **embodiment**, which is the way in which language affects the physical body but also how the body is used to communicate (including non-verbal communication such as gesture and facial expression). Following some trends in the wider gender/sexuality studies field, there's also an incipient trend to understand how emotion and **affect** relate to gender categories. In other words, even while it seems simple to note the performativity of gender, people nevertheless often genuinely 'feel' gender in various ways, through feeling discomfort (or comfort) in their own bodies, through feeling emotions that are 'authorized' or not for their category, and even by feeling a desire to be recognized performatively in a particular gender category. These are all important continuing questions arising from the new ways that the relationship between language and gender/sexuality is being conceived.

Added to these concerns are moves that are globalizing the field, with many studies that are both transnational in orientation and in location, located in global sites that do not figure prominently in the theorizing from North America and Europe from the last few decades. Such studies raise a slew of new questions about language and sexuality, including: How does the introduction of other regimes of embodiment such as skin color, body shape, ability, and so on affect the kinds of language used to engage with gender/sexuality performatively? To return to a version of a relatively old question in the field, what difference do these other embodied and affective categories make to gender, and what difference do all of the categories together make? These are questions that will no doubt begin to have answers in the next version of this book.

Notes

1 Haas was not only a pioneer in the description of American Indian Languages and in linguistic theory, she was also a pioneering woman in academia. It's worth looking up her Wikipedia page.
2 It's 'second wave' because the first wave were the suffragettes and others of the late 19th and early 20th century whose biggest accomplishment was getting women the right to vote in the US, as discussed in Chapter 3.
3 Linguists use the idea of **markedness** a lot, in the sense that one way of speaking will be an expected, more common, or unmarked way, while another will be the less expected, rare, or marked way. Lakoff is using this sense here, but also suggesting that feminine gender is marked ideologically as well.

References

Barrett, R. (1999). Indexing Polyphonous Identity in the Speech of African American Drag Queens. In Bucholtz, M., Liang, A. C., and Sutton, L. A., editors, *Reinventing Identities: The Gendered Self in Discourse*, pages 313–331. Oxford University Press, New York, NY.

Bucholtz, M. and Hall, K. (2004). Theorizing Identity in Language and Sexuality Research. *Language in Society*, 33:469–515.

Butler, J. (1990). *Gender Trouble: Feminism and the Subversion of Identity.* Routledge, New York, NY.

Cameron, D. (1998). "Is There Any Ketchup, Vera?": Gender, Power and Pragmatics. *Discourse & Society*, 9(4):437–455.

Cameron, D. and Kulick, D. (2003). *Language and Sexuality.* Cambridge University Press, New York, NY.

Cameron, D., McAlinden, F., and O'Leary, K. (1989). Lakoff in Context: The Social and Linguistic Functions of Tag Questions. In Coates, J. and Cameron, D., editors, *Women in Their Speech Communities*, pages 74–93. Longman, New York, NY.

Crenshaw, K. (1989). Demarginalizing the Intersection of Race and Sex: A Black Feminist Critique of Antidiscrimination Doctrine, Feminist Theory and Antiracist Politics. *University of Chicago Legal Forum, Special Issue: Feminism in the Law: Theory, Practice and Criticism*, pages 139–168. University of Chicago Law School, Chicago, IL.

Eckert, P. (1990). The Whole Woman: Sex and Gender Differences in Variation. *Language Variation and Change*, 1(1989):245–267.

Eckert, P. and McConnell-Ginet, S. (1992). Think Practically and Look Locally: Language and Gender as Community-based Practice. *Annual Review of Anthropology*, 21(1):461–490.

Fischer, J. L. J. (1958). Social Influences on the Choice of a Linguistic Variant. *Word*, 14(1):47–56.

Gramsci, A., Hoare, Q., and Nowell-Smith, G. (1971). *Selections from the Prison Notebooks of Antonio Gramsci.* International Publishers, New York, NY.

Gaudio, R. P. (1994). Sounding Gay: Pitch Properties in the Speech of Gay and Straight Men. *American Speech*, 69(1), 30–57.

Haas, M. (1944). Men's and Women's Speech in Koasati. *Language*, 20(3):142–149.

Hall, K. (1995). Lip Service on the Fantasy Lines. In Hall, K. and Bucholtz, M., editors, *Gender articulated: Language and the Socially Constructed Self*, pages 183–216. Routledge, New York, NY.

Hellinger, M. (1995). Language and Gender. In Stevenson, P., editor, *The German Language and the Real World*, pages 279–314. Oxford University Press, New York, NY.

Holmes, J. (1984). Hedging Your Bets and Sitting on the Fence: Some Evidence for Hedges as Support Structures. *Te Reo*, 27:47–62.

Holmes, J. (1995). *Women, Men and Politeness.* Longman, London.

Inoue, M. (2002). Gender, Language, and Modernity: Toward an Effective History of Japanese Women's Language. *American Ethnologist*, 29(2):392–422.

Irvine, J. and Gal, S. (2000). Language Ideology and Linguistic Differentiation. In Kroskrity, P. V., editor, *Regimes of Language: Ideologies, Polities, and Identities*, pages 35–84. School of American Research, Santa Fe, NM.

Jugaku, A. (1979). *Nihongo to onna (Japanese Language and Women)*. Iwanami Shoten, Tokyo.

Kulick, D. (2000). Gay and Lesbian Language. *Annual Review of Anthropology*, 29:243–285.

Labov, W. (1990). The Intersection of Sex and Social Class in the Course of Linguistic Change. *Language Variation and Change*, 2(2):205–254.

Lakoff, R. (1973). Language and Woman's Place. *Language in Society*, 2(1):45–80.

Lakoff, R. T. (1975). *Language and Woman's Place*. Harper & Row, New York, NY.

Leap, W. (1996). *Word's Out: Gay Men's English*. University of Minnesota Press, Minneapolis, MN.

Legman, G. (1941). The Language of Homosexuality: An American Glossary. In Henry, G. W., editor, *Sex Variants: A Study of Homosexual Patterns*, pages 1149–1179. Paul B. Hoeber, New York, NY.

Maltz, D. and Borker, R. (1982). A Cultural Approach to Male-Female Miscommunication. In Gumperz, J., editor, *Language and Social Identity*, pages 196–216. Cambridge University Press, Cambridge.

Moonwomon, B. (1997). Toward a Study of Lesbian Speech. In Livia, A. and Hall, K., editors, *Queerly Phrased: Language, Gender, and Sexuality*, pages 202–213. Oxford University Press, New York, NY.

Ochs, E. (1992). Indexing Gender. In Duranti, A. and Goodwin, C., editors, *Rethinking Context*, pages 335–358. Cambridge University Press, New York, NY.

Pusch, L. F. (1984). *Das Deutsche als Männersprache*. Suhrkamp, Frankfurt am Main.

Tannen, D. (1981). Indirectness in Discourse: Ethnicity as Conversational Style. *Discourse Processes*, 4(3):221–238.

Tannen, D. (1990). *You Just Don't Understand: Women and Men in Conversation*. William Morrow and Co., New York, NY.

Troemel-Ploetz, S. (1982). *Frauensprache: Sprache der Veränderung*, vol. 3725 edition. Fischer-Taschenbuch-Verlag, Frankfurt am Main.

Troemel-Ploetz, S. (1984). *Gewalt durch Sprache: Die Vergewaltigung vom Frauen in Gesprachen.* Fischer-Taschenbuch-Verlag, Frankfurt am Main.

Yukawa, S. and Saito, M. (2004). Cultural Ideologies in Japanese Language and Gender Studies. In Okamoto, S. and Smith, J. S. S., editors, *Japanese Language, Gender, and Ideology: Cultural Models and Real People*, pages 59–240. Oxford University Press, Oxford; New York, NY.

Chapter 5

Linguistic categorization and gender categories

Gender is a system of categories and language is a system for categorization. So, in this first of three main chapters, we'll look at how language creates, affects, and reflects gender/sexuality categories. You can see the power of language to categorize by thinking about how you would group items in your kitchen cabinet for round vessels that you use to put beverages, soups, salads, and cereal in. There is no doubt a large number of possible names for these vessels, such as *cup, bowl, glass, mug, vase*, and so on, and that's just a few terms in English. But where do you draw the line from cup to bowl? How wide or deep? What if there's a handle but it's wide and deep? This thought experiment is not just a naming exercise – it affects how you use things. Some vessels will be easy, because they look like the **prototype** – that is, the 'default' picture that comes to mind. If you have a wide round vessel (such as the one in Figure 5.1) with a handle and you put coffee in it, then you'll probably call it a mug. But if you put cereal in it, you will probably call it a bowl. In fact, William Labov (1973) showed that if you tell people to imagine different drinks and foods in the vessels, people will change where they draw the line between cup and bowl (see also Anderson and Prawat 1983). Moreover, if you call it a mug, then you're likely to use it for a drink. This is a simple but powerful example that shows how linguistic categorization affects how we think about and use things.

Gender is also a system of categorization. The social gender system actually originates in language: Many languages (including Old

Figure 5.1 A large cup or a small bowl?

English) have systems of categorizing nouns and speakers must change how they say things based on the 'gender' category of the noun (a difference in **morphology**, see Chapter 2). For example, in German, 'the cup' is *die Tasse*, while 'the mug' is *der Becher*. *Die* is used because *Tasse* is feminine and *der* is used because *Becher* is masculine. There's not really a rationale for things being masculine or feminine (although people try to make them up – is a mug more masculine than a cup?), and languages often differ on whether things are masculine or feminine (*moon* is masculine in German and feminine in French). Nevertheless, in these languages, every noun must have a category, and it rarely changes once the language settles on which category it belongs to.

Just as language creates categories through words and grammar, societies categorize people (gender, age, class, occupation, race, ethnicity, what kind of car you drive, etc.). These systems are obviously a lot more complicated than the linguistic ones (at least it seems that way), because things like status get attached to them. But the important point is that language has many resources for categorizing things, and this power of categorization helps societies create social categories. This chapter explains some of the main ways that languages create and reflect the social category of gender.

Gender is of course the main social category we are worried about in this book, and we've already explored that category a lot in Chapter 3. But just for a moment, just to show how society and language categorization can get entwined, let's use an example from another system of categorizing people: race. In the US, racial categories tend to be organized around Black and White, and each of those categories come with stereotypes, including how people speak. There is no inherent reason to categorize people in this way, and language helps to create the categories. Sometimes cracks appear in the system when it meets reality. For example, Benjamin Bailey (2002) shows how Dominicans in the US complicate these racial categories. Dominicans tend to be recognized as Black by how they look, but they speak Spanish, and in the US, *Black* and *Hispanic* are usually considered mutually exclusive categories, so this combination of language and appearance leads to confusion. In another example, in South Africa under apartheid, the language used for racial categories was very different than in the US (the South African categories are still used today but defined differently): Black, Coloured [sic], Indian/Asian, and White.[1] These two examples show that there is nothing inherent in the criteria for racial categories, how many categories are named, or where the boundaries are among the categories. So the racial group naming systems are as arbitrary as whether to call something a *cup* or *bowl*, and are based on history and society rather than biology or language. Nevertheless, once these naming systems are in place, they are powerful, and have significant effects on people's lives. The terms are more than 'just a word.'

As we saw in Chapter 3, gender categorization is central to the maintenance of a gender system – without the two clear categories opposed to one another, there is no system. You might think that it is as simple as masculine-feminine, male-female, he-she. But the powers of categorization are not just naming and choosing – people *use* those categories and their content in interaction, when we talk to each other. In fact, we learn the meanings of most word categories through interaction. For example, when you were a child, adults and older children referred to cups, mugs, bowls, and so on, over and over again (or similar terms in your native language if not English), and you learned the boundaries from all that interaction. The same is true for gender, but the important characteristics are far more complex, and have far more impact on people's lives, than the decision about whether something is a cup or bowl.

In this chapter, then, we'll explore some of the ways language categorization works with gender categorization. I write "works with" because the connection is not necessarily causal in any direction: language categorization neither simply creates nor simply reflects gender categorization. Rather, they work together to create and sustain systems of gender categorization in societies. Linguistic gender categorization is an inherent part of the gender system. As we saw above, that categorization is also involved in societal systems of power. So rather than simply looking at how language divides the world by gender, we will also explore how that division creates power differences among people of different genders, sexualities, and other identities. We begin with systems of grammar themselves.

Gender in grammar: Is language sexist?

We've already touched slightly on gender in English pronouns: *he/him/his*, *she/her/hers*, *it/its*. The choice of pronoun is sometimes an identity and political issue, and we will discuss this issue in English below. But first, let's consider some even more general issues of how languages encode social categories in their grammars, starting with Japanese. One of the hardest things about learning Japanese as a second (or later) language is that it has a fairly complex system of **honorifics**. Honorifics are words that change depending on the status of the people you are talking to or referring to. In Japanese, you have to pay attention to the relative status of yourself as speaker to both the people you talk about and the people you talk to, and their gender as well. It can get very involved – I'll spare you the details (if you're interested, have a look at the Wikipedia page for "Japanese Honorifics"). The point is that in order to really speak Japanese, you need to pay attention to the honorific categories. So grammars of languages encode the social order in which they are used and force people to pay attention to the categories encoded; you can't really become a fluent speaker of Japanese if you don't know what kinds of status categories to pay attention to in the society. For example, it's not just about hierarchy, but also about whether a person is more or less a member of a relevant social group you belong to (there is a non-honorific "plain style," but my Japanese-speaking friends tell me that you sound like a child if you use it).

The same goes for gender categories in many languages. In English, in order to use a third person pronoun, for example, you need to know whether you're dealing with *he*, *she*, *it*, or *they*. So first you need to know whether you are referring to singular or plural (*they* vs. everything else). If singular, you need to know if you are referring to something that is human(-ish) or not (*it* vs. *he/she*), and finally, if human, what that human's gender is. Other languages take this further, because in languages like German, for example, you need to use different articles and endings if, for example, your teacher is a woman (*die Lehrerin*) or a man (*der Lehrer*).

So what's the issue with having categories? Can grammar be **sexist**? *Sexist* is usually a term we use for people, but we can extend it to grammatical systems of language. In general, people use *sexist* to mean that there is some way gender is involved in a power asymmetry, especially systematically (we might find that gender is always involved in power asymmetry, but that's a different argument). There are a few main ways that grammar ends up being sexist, but they all end up privileging the masculine in some way. The most obvious and pervasive is the 'masculine default' or 'generic masculine' in which, for example, *he/him/his* is used for mixed gender. Imagine that this is a statement on a syllabus at a university attended by both men and women:

(1) Every student must turn off his phone in class.

This is a **generic** statement, meaning it is true all the time, and for every student. The *his* is meant to refer to any student, male or female. This use is sexist because it sets up men as the default option. One way that a system of power difference between men and women is maintained is by creating an ideology where women seem somehow 'less than human' or 'childlike,' because in the gender ideology, to be fully human means to be a man.

It's important to realize that the main argument that this is sexist is not necessarily to do with whether anyone thinks of a man when this sentence or ones like it are uttered (although there is plenty of evidence that this is the case; see, for example, Hamilton 1988). Rather, it is about the system of language and categorization that speakers must pay attention to. In other words, you can't really understand the above sentence if you don't access men as the default category. The effect is to send a message that suggests men are the default humans and women are somehow different or odd or not fully human.

English also does not have a non-gendered human term: you have to choose *his* or *her*. In this way, the linguistic system works with gender ideology to make it impossible to have a generic non-gendered human. In casual speech, *they* is used commonly (see Newman 1997, Baranowski 2002, and Balhorn 2004). In fact, both generic *he* and *they* have been part of English since Old English (so, basically as long as we have records of English), as outlined by Anne Curzan (2003). Curzan shows how both forms coexisted for centuries, even as English lost its grammatical gender system (that is, one like German). It wasn't until grammarians began to **prescribe** language in the 18th century that a 'rule' 'was developed to use generic *he* at the expense of *they*, although Curzan notes (2003, pp. 73–79) that there was significant disagreement about such a rule and especially its details. The point here is that generic *he* and *they* have been in competition for centuries, and that there is certainly no reason that *he* or even *he or she* (or *s/he* or *she or he*, etc.) is more 'natural.'

Of course, as discussed in Chapter 4, language changes, and the generic use of the plural *they* seems to gathering steam, so it is now unremarkable to read the following:

(2) Every student must turn off their phone in class.

More significantly, there is a nascent movement to complete the removal of gender from English pronouns altogether with the use of *they* for all third person contexts. Such a shift would leave only two third person pronouns in English: *it* and *they*. For example, in the following example, *they/their* would refer to Jordan (the subscript 'i' is how linguists show that pronouns are **coindexed** to each other, meaning they refer to the same entity):

(3) As Jordan$_i$ scrubbed their$_i$ hands before surgery, they$_i$ reviewed the procedure mentally.

There are other ways that English and other languages set up the masculine as the default, and thus more powerful, category. For example, in the German above, note that the feminine term is longer and appears derived from the masculine: *Lehrerin* vs. *Lehrer*. Linguists call the longer term the **marked** term, and the shorter the **unmarked**. We can generalize from this to notice that feminine terms tend to be more marked than masculine, thus creating a whole system in which the masculine is more default than the feminine.

As recently as the 1980s, English had more such marked feminine terms, such as *stewardess* and *actress*. It's remarkable that this shift has occurred in the short span of about 50 years (usually linguistic change is not so swift). In some cases, a new generic term was created, such as *flight attendant* in the case of *stewardess*. In others, however, the unmarked term just became the one used for everyone. In general, this is true for *actor*, although *actress* is still used by many, especially in awards such as the Academy Awards, in which there are separate awards for actor and actress. (Note that this is the only social category that affects the awards – there's no separate Best Black Actor award – and that all other categories such as director and costume design don't have separate gender categories!) Finally, we can see the masculine-as-default through the ways that (usually prestigious) terms are modified for feminine but not masculine. The most common example is to note that doctor (at least historically) was often modified as *woman doctor* (or even *lady doctor*), a term that shows that the default is *man doctor*. Once again, this practice is less common now than even 20 years ago.

Even attempts to equalize such defaults can meet resistance. For example, the term *chairman* and *congressman* are usually changed to *chair/chairperson* and *congressperson* (although often *congressman* and *congresswoman* are kept if discussing a specific person and their gender is known). In these cases, the non-gendered generic term some- times ends up being used only for feminine holders of the office and not the male, so that in the end the asymmetry is maintained. For exam- ple, a chairperson is a woman, but a chairman, a man. So language categorization sets up the generic as masculine and it is marked if a feminine person is fulfilling that category.

This is an asymmetry, and asymmetries are the hallmark of power differences. Sometimes, the asymmetry can become so distinct that the words come to mean very different things, not just a feminine ver- sion of the masculine term. For example, *master* and *mistress* used to be parallel terms in English: they both denoted the heads of the household, or more generally a leader of family/clan/etc. But over the centuries, the meaning of *mistress* changed to mean an illicit hetero-sexual lover of a (often powerful) married man. *Master* retained, and arguably increased, its associations with power. There are other such differences, some more subtle such as *lord/lady* and *king/queen*.

In both vocabulary and grammar, then, languages do lots to encode gender binaries. Once created, they tend to end up being asymmetrical, reflecting and helping to perpetuate the power imbalances in the gender ideology of a society. While you might think this is abstract grammar thinking, categories are used frequently by speakers in interaction, and it is here that they have their greatest power. We consider how this happens in the next section.

Gender and sexual identity categorization in interaction

While the system of language – its categories, pronouns, rules of word order, and so on – can organize things by gender and in a sexist way, it is really in the *use* of categories in interaction and the assumptions made by speakers about what other speakers will recognize that is important.[2] Let's take a pretty straightforward example from an article by Emanuel Schegloff (1997, pp. 180–182). One of the interesting things about this example is that in this article, Schegloff is arguing against the idea that interactions should be analyzed to see how the identities of the interact-ants affect how they are doing the interaction (a topic we address in the next chapter). Rather, the idea is that people will in different ways **orient** themselves to different identity categories. While Schegloff's proposal in its most extreme form is controversial, he does include an example that shows how interactants can do this orienting to gender in interaction. In this example, a group is having dinner and one person asks for the but-ter, and then two more ask if they "can have some too." The first person says "no," then after a short pause says, "Ladies last," which is an inver-sion of a common saying in American English, "Ladies first," as well as an actual common practice of letting women take the first turn in many social instances, especially in dining situations. At this point, you know that the requesters were probably women, and the first speaker has made this relevant by using this phrase. Moreover, by making that distinction, you probably inferred that this speaker is a man.

All of this is brought up by the simple phrase of *ladies last*. So this use of *ladies* is more than simply recognizing that the speaker is talking to women, but rather it embeds the category in the interaction in a significant way that also pulls out aspects of gender ideologies. In this example, we also see how language categories are used by speakers beyond their simple identification or dictionary definition purposes. So even everyday uses of *woman* and *man* make gender relevant, and certainly other ways of referring to gendered beings as well (even questions about a dog's sex).

Another example is analyzed by Elizabeth Stokoe (2006), who shows that a group of college students use gender as a **warrant** to assign a "scribe" for their small group discussion. In this instance, one of the men in the four-person group nominates the only woman in the group by saying "She wants to do it," and then, "Secretary and female." He thereby uses the ideological connection between secretaries and women as a warrant to assign the woman the relatively subservient role as secretary. This utterance doesn't even make sense unless you can access the ideological connection between the job of secretary and femininity (and possibly the more general association with women and service positions), which the woman apparently does as she takes up her pen to be the scribe. This is a particularly powerful way that language is used to categorize, because even if you don't share the idea that 'women should be secretaries,' you have to access that ideology (or what we will see called later **cultural models**) in order for it to make sense.

Similarly, Stokoe cites some other examples of assault suspects who deny that they assaulted women by saying that as a general rule they would never hit or physically assault a woman. Here again, these don't make sense as denial unless you can access the idea that women are more delicate or should not be physically assaulted by a man – or even more so, that an 'honorable man' would never physically assault a woman. And the speakers being interrogated are counting on this understanding (at least implicitly) in order to convince the interrogator that they did not hit the women.

Implicit reference to sexual orientation and sexual identity is arguably even more common, probably because the assumption of heterosexuality is more of a default category than any gender category. That is, in general and especially if people are relatively unknown to them, people make assumptions that the people they are talking to are hetero-sexual, and these assumptions are reflected in linguistic use patterns. Let's look at an example of this kind of categorization in interaction, adapted from a discussion by Celia Kitzinger (2005), who has pub-lished several studies on this topic. She especially focuses on interac-tional constructions of heterosexuality, that is, "how people produce themselves and others as heterosexual and – in so doing – constitute a normative heterosexual world" (Kitzinger 2005, p. 228). She shows that there are a number of ways that this heterosexual identification happens **covertly**, that is, as a secondary meaning and not the main focus of the interaction, whereas this kind of unremarkable reference is not so easily accomplished when referring to homosexual relationships.

There are several ways she finds that this happens. The first is by reference to 'another half' – married heterosexual categories of *hus-band* and *wife*. So, if I say, "I'm calling to make an appointment for my wife," that relationship is clear, but if I say (in a recognizably mascu-line voice), "I'm calling to make an appointment for my husband," then there is often a disfluency in response. Kitzinger provides examples in which the sexuality of the relationships 'hijacks' the whole interaction in these cases (see Land and Kitzinger [2005] for examples). A similar process happens if someone refers to a person through their relation-ship with a known person in interaction. For example, if someone says, "Quin's wife fell down the other day," there's both an assumption that the hearer knows Quin but also that they don't know his wife (and he is a masculine person). So the use of *wife* is significant because theoreti-cally Quin's wife has a name of her own (see also Sidnell [2003] for a similar case in Guyanese Creole).

The second way sexuality works in interaction is through identifica-tion of a couple with pronouns. For example, someone might ask me, "How's your new house?" and I might respond "It's a mess. We're renovating the entire basement." Kitzinger shows that in situations like this, once again conversations continue smoothly when the *we* refer-ence is a heterosexual couple, but not necessarily when it is not. In addition, in interaction, once one member of a couple has been intro-duced, often the 'other half' can be referred to simply as a gendered pronoun. For example, if Mrs. Hooper has been introduced (crucially using *Mrs.*, which marks her as married), a simple *he* might be used to refer to Mr. Hooper.

Such labeling of **ratified categories** has effects for other non-stereotypical relationships. For example, in American English, people who are in committed heterosexual relationships but aren't married, especially if they are older than about their 30s, have problematic reference options. So, for example, *boyfriend* and *girlfriend* tend to clash with both the age of the people in the couple (they're not boys or girls) and commitment level of the relationship (it's not casual or short-term). As Kitzinger suggests in other contexts, perhaps *partner* is an option, but that seems to miss the closeness and sounds more like a business partnership (and for some people, it indexes a homosexual relationship, which is not a true representation of the relationship). So you can see that that the normativity of heterosexual relationships, while most strongly encoding the heterosexual, also codes other aspects of the people involved in the relationships and how they relate to the expected life course of a person (the situation above is odd because there's an expectation that people get married when they are of a certain age, and also if the relationship is serious they get married, and only once at that; older people aren't expected to be boyfriends and girlfriends and in fact younger people, say, of college age, aren't expected to be husband and wife). Just as in Kitzinger's example, there's a sizeable minority of people who don't fit the normative script, and no terms have developed to name these relationships. We'll see this sort of coding again a little later when we discuss the role of the lexicon in semantic scripts.

Gender and figurative language

Gendered metaphors

One of the joys of using language is that one can be so creative, and that is nowhere as clear as with using **figures of speech**, especially the description of men or women using **metaphors**. There are quite a few of these just in English. You might want to investigate the kinds of animal metaphors you see used (or generate a list with friends), for example, with women referred to as *birds* or *chicks*, but also *cow* and *bitch*. Hines (1999) provides an interesting study of this phenomenon in English (with helpful lists), arguing that one important organizing metaphor about women is WOMEN ARE SMALL ANIMALS (I'm not shouting: there's a convention in studying metaphor to write the metaphor in all caps). But Hines points out that not all small animals will do, and some animals are actually used as insults to women. For example, *bunny* is widespread, but *hare* is never used. Hines argues that the reason is that *hare* does not fit the kinds of 'sound shape' or phonology that these words tend to have. Namely, they tend to have initial consonants in this set: [p, b, f, k, g, and tʃ] (the last sound in that list is the sound at the beginning of *chick*). These are tendencies and are affected by both sound and meaning; *puppy* fits the sound pattern, but dogs are generally not associated with women, except as an insult. So *puppy*, even though a young animal and the sound pattern fits, isn't used as a metaphor for women. In general, for the semantics of these metaphors, there has to be some way in which ideologies about animals aligns with ideologies about women. There has been less research about similar masculine terms as feminine ones, but it's interesting to note that *dog* is used for men, but usually in a way that suggests connection or solidarity among men. For example, among many men in the US, one could even use it as an address term (sometimes spelled *dawg*).

People draw on gender categories widely for metaphorical work because gender ideologies are so widely shared. The metaphors can work in the opposite direction when the adverbial connotations of masculinity or femininity are used to describe or add qualities to objects. The example of my son saying that a vehicle was particularly masculine is a good example. In this case, it was a *Hummer*, which was originally a military vehicle and is large and has sharp edges and looks particularly indestructible. So rather than saying "That is a particularly large, intimidating and physically powerful-looking vehicle," my son simply said, "That's a masculine-looking car." In fact, cars are often mentioned in terms that have gendered implications, partially because there are ideas about what gender stereotypically drives such cars (trucks are more masculine, VW Beetles are more feminine).

A **simile** that has been used creatively and has even become a bone of cultural contention in the English-speaking world lately is the metaphor of *throw like a girl*.[3] The idea is that there is a particular way that girls throw, which is different from boys. There is an identifiable motion that is the supposed 'girl-throw,' but it is generally the way a human throws without training.[4] Nevertheless, we're not so much concerned with the physicality of the term, but the way it is used metaphorically. That is, someone might say, "You throw like a girl" as a way of saying someone is physically awkward or weak. This phrase has taken on a life of its own, and even been reclaimed by some women (with the point that girls are strong and athletic). But it shows one of the ways that ideologies about gender can get recruited interactionally and then are used to reinforce that ideology. You may even want to discuss whether using the phrase to empower women might do the opposite, since in order to even understand what it means, you have to call to mind the stereotype that views girls (and women) as weaker as less physically talented.[5] There are countless such metaphors, and since humans are creative, new ones are developed constantly. Let's consider just a few more. We'll explore not just the metaphors, but also how they are used and expanded.

Before you move on, a warning. In the rest of this chapter, I cite a lot of language that some people find offensive. But linguists look at language as it is used in the real world, and these words and terms are used. More importantly, I think that they are powerful ways that gender ideologies are perpetuated, and that hiding them won't do us any good. Just to be clear, I'm not trying to insult you or use them to insult, but presenting them as objects to be studied (similar to the way that doctors might study drawings of unclothed bodies in a way that is non-sexual or offensive). All right, you've been warned.

Naming of parts

Before you read this section in full, especially if you need a break from reading, you might want to go do the following activity with your friends. It's based on one devised by Deborah Cameron (1992) who writes about a class project (which arose from a class discussion) in which one group of men and one group of women listed as many terms as they could think of for *penis*. (Here's where you would want to stop reading and go make your own lists, to see how it compares with the ones Cameron's students produced.)

The lists produced (provided in full in the article) are revealing for a number of reasons. Cameron took both lists and categorized the terms

that were used. The group of men produced 144 terms. The first category was personal names, which as Cameron points out is part of the
way that men sometimes talk about their penis as if it is a separate
person from them, which is problematic because it feeds into ideas of
uncontrollable urges and rape. Nevertheless, most of the names were
various powerful figures, although a subgroup was also one that was
basically nicknames (like *Johnson*). Other categories included animal
names (powerful or serpentine), tools (with similar shapes, commonly
power tools), weapons/firearms, and food (mainly of a similar shape),
a small group referring metaphorically to insertion into a body part,
phonological wordplay, and a random group that included references
to other body parts and size or shape. The women's list was rather different (and shorter) and left out the categories of "authority symbols,
ravening beasts, tools, and weapons. One might generalize by saying
that women find the penis endearing, ridiculous, and occasionally dis-
gusting, but not awe-inspiring or dangerous" (1992, p. 374). The lists
show not only different conceptions of body parts, but also different
conceptions of the sex act. Because of the taboo nature of this activity,
it's kind of fun, but even though both groups approached the task with
humor, Cameron points out that "they must in the end reaffirm the
values they have dared to joke about. When a man suggests so baroque
a term as, say, *purple helmeted love warrior* for his penis, he partly
distances himself from the metaphors of penis-as-hero and sex-as-war;
but partly, too, he recirculates those metaphors" (1992, p. 374). The
different conceptions of sex, says Cameron (1992, p. 379), express "an
experience of masculinity as dominance, femininity as passivity, and
sex as conquest." So, the "naming of parts" is more than just naming,
but rather brings in larger ideologies about gender and sex. Braun and
Kitzinger (2001) find similar results. If you do decide to have some
friends do this activity (or your instructor asks you to), then you might
think about comparing your lists with these. Are there different categories? If they are similar, are they present in similar proportions?
What comments did your friends make while doing this activity? What
results do you get for similar lists for vagina?

This research (and the activity) shows how much social and linguistic
effort goes into thinking about gendered bodies. Lal Zimman's (2014)
exploration of genital terminology among transmasculine people shows

how the use of terms is more than a straightforward description of bodily 'facts.'[6] Rather, Zimman finds that even terms as clinical and 'descriptive' as *penis* and *clitoris* are available for reconfiguration in talk. The actual anatomical truth is that the clitoris and penis are **homologous** organs, meaning that, in short (and simplifying considerably), a penis is a large clitoris (or a clitoris is a small penis), and both start out as the same prenatal structure. In fact, there are many people born with indeterminate structures which are often reshaped soon after birth to fit with normative ideas about binary sex (see Blackless et al. 2000 and Preves 2002 for more on the topic). Zimman shows that "Trans speakers question the reasoning that says particular physiological characteristics are inherently gendered, contesting the assumption that having a penis necessarily makes a body male while having a vagina (or lacking a penis) makes a body female" (2014, p. 23). For example, the trans men that Zimman talks to frequently use the vernacular terms *dick* and *cock* to refer to their external genitals, no matter the physical shape and appearance of the appendage. In this way, they refigure their gender and even what might be conventionally called *sex* (see Chapter 3), showing even more the power of language to categorize and organize experience.

Insults

Many of the names for parts we've just talked about are also used as insulting terms for people, which leads us to a consideration of how gendered and sexual insults are used differently, whether they are based on women, men, or 'non-hegemonic' sexualities.[7] There's actually another good party game, or class activity, involving these words. That is: Have a group of people generate a list of profanity, and then have them sort the list based on how 'strong' the profanity is. Are there any patterns? I'm willing to bet that lower down are religious terms (*damn*, *hell*, etc.) and scatological terms (*poop*, *shit*, *piss*, etc.), while as the severity increases, so do references to sex and anatomy, and on or near the top is the term *cunt*. In fact, recently in the US, there's been quite a controversy about one comedian's use of this word.[8] It's important to note that there are many other terms that would not have even caused anyone to comment, but *cunt*, used by a woman to another woman, caused a kerfuffle.

If you made a list, it's worth exploring some of the ways your list works, but in general, it's revealing that terms for sex (*fuck*) and for sexual body parts (*cock* and *cunt*) are at the top, and that the slang term for a female body part, in which that part is arguably most sexualized, is at the top of so many lists. This fact suggests that women's sexual desire (and especially an agentive sexual desire) is the most taboo. This taboo is also true of insulting slang terms categorizing women such as *bitch* and especially *whore* and *slut*, for which there are no equivalent masculine terms; that is, an insult which can be leveled at a man for being too sexually promiscuous. The strength and whether or not the term is an insult is dependent on when they are used and who uses them with whom. For example, *cunt* seems to be more likely to be used by men to insult other men, while for women it is sometimes used as a term of solidarity (see McEnery [2004] for the data for the UK which shows this pattern). So it is perceived as particularly strong when a woman uses *cunt* to insult another woman. So again, language categorizes not by being a system that is 'out there' or 'in the dictionary,' but through the ways people use the language, with whom, and in what situation. (Another good example, which I don't have space for, is the use of *bitch boy* by the fraternity members I studied; see Kiesling 2002.)

Such insults are not limited to English or the US. A recent article by Zhuo Jing-Schmidt and Xinxia Peng (2018) discusses a new form used on the Chinese microblogging platform (similar to Twitter) Weibo. The form, 婊 *biǎo*, means literally 'female prostitute,' but is used more like *slut*. Moreover, it is used as a suffix to simply mean 'bad woman,' usually without the sexual or economic meanings of prostitution (although sometimes one of those valences is part of the negativity). The article explores much of the fascinating and complicated way that this word is being used, but for our purposes, the important point is that the suffix is added especially when the main root word refers to women "who strive for values of goodness, dignity, and empowerment" (2018, p. 396). Moreover, the suffix is spreading so that it is used in terms that refer to men, which means that an inherently feminine-marked word is becoming simply a marker of negative character, which recapitulates the idea that masculine is good and pure and strong and feminine is weak and conniving. Such categorization is often subtle not only in this case, but in other cases, including those I turn to next.

Categorization of normative sexuality and intimacy

As we saw in Chapter 3, there is a host of terms for different configurations of gender identity and sexual identity apart from the actual desires that go on in people's minds and bodies (although one of the ideologies is that there is a causal connection there). But there are also normative models that are widely shared (even if resisted) in a culture or community, and these are reflected in the ways that people label others. In this section, I'll look at two ways that language recapitulates a normatively heterosexual path of intimacy. This first has to do with the way that language is used to categorize men in American English, while the second is the word *marriage*. Dorothy Holland and Debra Skinner (1987) investigated how terms used to describe men at a university in the southern US organized the ways that the women categorized men, such as *jock, chauvinist pig, dude, athlete, hunk, playboy, turkey, nerd, jerk, wimp, sissy, man, guy, gentleman, sweetheart, boyfriend*, among many others. They started with an extensive list and tried categorizing at the different dimensions of meaning, such as being good-looking, etc. But they also did extensive interviews and discovered that the terms really made sense when they were thought of as comparing a man with a prototypical one in a standard **cultural model** of intimacy.

In this model, crucially, men and women were compared in terms of prestige, usually deriving from appearance. Further, according to the model, a man must treat a woman well – do things that show she is special – in order to win her affection (and intimacy). This will probably be familiar as an ideology of 'the man in pursuit of the woman.' But prestige is not always matched, and in those cases, a man who has higher prestige may not treat the woman well or she may provide affection without that good treatment, or both. Similarly, if the woman has higher prestige, the man must treat the woman in an extra special way. Holland and Skinner found that the terms for men implicitly refer to these relationships. So, for example, *nerds* and *wimps* don't know how to treat a woman and may be otherwise prestige-challenged. *Don Juans* are highly prestigious and don't treat women well. And, of course, men who don't fit in to the heterosexual pattern of the model are marked as well (as *gay* or *queer*). So these terms are more than dictionary definitions, but understandable only with reference to this normative pattern of sexuality.

Marriage is similarly normative (indeed, it is the final stage of model above, in which the man becomes a *husband*; it would be interesting to explore the cultural models for older heterosexual couples rather than those in college). McConnell-Ginet (2006) shows that debates about the definition of marriage in the US are a significant activity that is more than 'mere semantics.' Rather, these discussions relate to the cultural model of marriage and it fits into the wider culture as an institution in terms of right and responsibilities. For our purposes, it's important to notice the ways in which a word such as *marriage* is related to a category and categories, but has important social consequences. One point McConnell-Ginet makes, which hearkens back to Chapter 4 on linguistics, is that *marriage* means different things in different cultures, and in fact has had different meanings in European history. For example, there was a time in much of the world in which marriage meant a relationship, essentially, of property, with the wife being the equivalent of the husband's property. Moreover, marriage was an economic contract before it was a religious one in Christian-dominated countries, so it didn't result 'naturally' from religion. And until 1967 in the US, interracial marriage was banned in many states (such prohibitions were struck down as unconstitutional in 1967).

So as cultural models of intimacy change (and you can compare your words for men and women with the above to see if anything has changed or is different in your language and culture), so does the meaning that a term like *marriage* encodes, and arguments about its definition are important and significant, as we saw earlier in this chapter with the usefulness of terms such as *husband* and *wife*. One important recent change is the definition of sexual consent in marriage, which only recently has become possible to even talk about, as it was long legally recognized that marriage was tacit blanket consent for sexual intercourse. This observation suggests that ideas about what counts as *sexual consent* and *rape* have also changed, and I turn to that next.

Categorization of sexual violence

Gender and sexual ideologies have probably their most serious consequence when it comes to how cultures understand issues of **sexual consent** and **rape**. I discuss some of the more important consequences of gender in interaction with respect to rape in the next chapter, but here I want to suggest that the normative model of pursuit by a man of a woman is important in how rape has been conceptualized and even legally defined.

Rape is a crime, and as such has to be defined legally. Generally, rape is defined as some kind of sexual penetration without consent of one party. The definition of **sexual consent** then becomes the most important definitional issue. The problem is that in the cultural model above, it may be difficult to determine what *consent* actually means. As Kulick (2003) points out in a classic article on the word *no*, refusal is often taken to mean something more like 'not yet,' which in the cultural model articulated above might be understood as an invitation to 'treat me really really well and I might change my mind.' And, as Kulick further points out, *no* might actually be heard as *yes*. So *consent* is a word that describes an interactional process – consent or refusal may not be contained in a single utterance. But we agree and disagree in many different ways in interaction, which makes the definition of consent to be problematic. Moreover, consent might be given because you fear the consequences of not giving it; if someone is threatening your life or even other sorts of pain and embarrassment, you may agree to all sorts of things (and the threat may not even be explicit, or the person may not even mean an action as a threat for it to be taken that way).

For consent in rape cases, the definition of a refusal often has an impossibly high bar, in which the person raped will be expected to have resisted to their utmost ability, rather than submitting through fear (or, also possible, conditioning through fear because of previous instances of rape). There is much to explore here (see Ehrlich et al. [2016] for a recent collection of articles on the topic), but the important point is to understand that the categorization of consent is not a straightforward 'dictionary' definition, and that such definitional struggles have serious consequences both in the behavior of the rapist and for justice.

More recently in the US, since the 1990s the circulation of the term **sexual harassment** has been important in (slowly) making institutions more equal for women. The activities that fall under the term sexual harassment have probably always existed, but in most cases, it was not seen as a problem, but rather 'normal operating procedure.' It was important, then, especially once women and men began studying and working together more often, that the term *sexual harassment*

developed and circulated. The term has taken a long road to acceptance, and I suggest that it's not unrelated to the cultural models of
intimacy and definitions of rape discussed previously. That is, if one
carries a cultural model in which men pursue desirable women and
women resist intimacy in order to extract good treatment, unwanted
sexual advances by men with power follow rather naturally. Using the
term *sexual harassment* changes the rules and creates a category in
which this model is not legitimate. So it is an important concept, but
one that is up against other ideologies of sexual relationships which are
still being worked out in American and no doubt other cultures. In this
case, language has had the power to change categories for the good,
even if only somewhat.

The politics of pronouns and binarity

Given the power of categorization to affect lives and people's being,
it's not odd that terms and names have been important and controversial for people who don't feel that they fit into any of those categories,
much as the pronoun *they* has been increasingly adopted by people
who don't feel they fit into *he* or *she*. But pronouns are only the beginning. There is, to put it mildly, more than one way to feel that one's
experience does not fit into the language that categorizes it. As we've
seen, one of the powers of language is that it can force a normativity
on its speakers – forcing people to be described as *women* or *men*,
for example. So it's been important to people who don't fit into the
normative language to think carefully, and sometimes contentiously,
about what terms to use to describe themselves. I've used a number
of these terms already in this book, often using my own description
(depending on the categorization desired) but more often defaulting to
the language used by the speakers themselves or the author who knows
them best.

One of the reasons that the **initialization** for non-hegemonic sexualities (**LGBTQIA+**) is so ever expanding is that there are so many ways
to experience sexuality.[9] The initialization first known as **LGB** was
formed because there was need for a term that referred to non-hegemonic sexualities and sexual identities. *Gay* generally only referred to
men, and *lesbian* to women. The 'LG' was meant to include them both,

while **bisexual** covers people who don't fall into either category. As these don't cover **transsexual** and **transgender** identities, it was common for 'T' to be added. But what if you are none of these but still don't think of yourself as normatively heterosexual? Well, that's why a lot of the other letters got added: 'Q' which is variously suggested to be either **questioning** or **Queer** (more on that word in a moment), 'I' for **intersex** (see Chapter 3) and 'A,' which itself can cover a lot of categories such as **allies** (people who aren't in these categories but are supportive of their causes), **asexual, aromantic, or agender**.[10] The {a-} prefix means *without*, so it is used with several categories of people who don't think of themselves as marked in a particular identity dimension. While this acronymic proliferation might seem excessive, the whole point is that it is describing people who have been invisible and not included in sexual and identity categorizations at all for most of history. Even my term *non-hegemonic* or even *non-normative* is problematic in the way it negatively defines the category. So there's a tension here that is unlikely to be resolved, but it's useful to use the right initialization depending on the actual reference group. For example, if one is only talking about gay and lesbian men and women, then just use those terms. Above, we noted that the categories that language encoded were almost invisible since they were so banal. The terms I've just been discussing are the opposite and try to diminish the power of these unmarked terms by making them visible through names for alternative categories.

The word and category **Queer** seems like a useful catch-all term that avoids negativity, but it was originally used as a very strong slur, mostly for homosexual people, and because of this history it is problematic as a positive term. So even though it has been **reclaimed** and is often used by members of what we might call a Queer community, *queer* still has its history and power to be heard as an insult and even a threat.[11] You may also encounter the term **Queer Theory** (see Jagose 1996), which is a way of talking about all sorts of literary, performance, and social issues from a perspective that challenges the hegemonic connections among gender, sexuality, and sexual identity. In my understanding, the main point in Queer Theory is destabilization and questioning of such categories. In fact, our exploration of how linguistic categories influence the ways in which communities conceive of such categories is influenced by Queer Theory (recall Judith Butler's ideas about performativity from Chapter 3).[12]

Finally, let's look at some of the issues of categorization in the 'T' part of the initialization. This letter stands for words beginning with *trans*, a term that generally stands for **transgender** or **transsexual**, which refers in different ways to people whose gender identity does not match the gender assigned when they were born. Transgender is generally the more widely used and accepted term, as explained in Gay and Lesbian Alliance Against Defamation (2018); there are also other terms which reflect different ways of thinking about gender within this community, see Zimman 2017). In a similar sense as Queer, **Trans** is a term that is somewhat contested and not always specific. You will see some writers add an asterisk to Trans: **Trans***. This is meant to be more inclusive, but some in the community believe that Trans is already inclusive enough and have other objections (some as simple as "how do you say that?"). The important fact is that this debate occurs in the community it describes – the terms are not imposed on people but rather developed by them based on how they as a community wish to include or exclude. Such interactions are difficult and fraught, but ultimately show the power of language to create important social categories and empower as well as denigrate.

Woman, man

To finish this chapter, let's come back to the binary that we talked about at the beginning: the distinction between the categories, *man/masculinity* and *woman/femininity*, and consider those as our last foray into categorization. Indeed, it is one of the main categories used by Lévi-Strauss (1958) to argue for structural anthropology, a theory (to simplify) in which all categories are binary and exist only insofar as they are opposites of another. So *woman* exists as 'not *man*,' and vice-versa; neither exists without the 'opposite.' There is a sense in which things that are not recognized as masculine are deemed feminine (although this may not be true in the other direction, something you may want to discuss).

But there are other ways that gender intersects with other categories and even takes on a tinge of them. Recall the discussions of

intersectionality in Chapters 3 and 4, in which it is argued that categories combine in unpredictable ways when they exist in the same person. Moreover, generic gender categories end up implying other aspects of identity such as class and race. For example, prototypical men (the one you think of when someone just says, "this man") in the US tend to be more likely to be seen as working class, while prototypical women are more likely to be imagined as middle to upper class. And both categories are often assumed to be White. So even though these categories are not marked for class or race, it is true that the generic conceptions of woman and man are often conceived with class and race as defaults, or rather they exist in an unmarked category that is widely shared. In fact, although somewhat awkward, I've been starting to use the terms **feminine people** and **masculine people** rather than women and men, respectively. This chapter has only scratched the categorization surface, but you should be able to see some of the ways that language and language users categorize people (and thoughts and activities) in terms of gender and sexuality, and some of the consequences for that categorization, whether they are social, psychological, or political.

Notes

1 See http://politicsweb.co.za/news-and-analysis/the-strange-career-of-race-classification-in-south.
2 This observation could take you into a nice discussion of the ways words have meaning, and you could look into the ideas of Wittgenstein and "language games," but I don't have space for it in this short introduction.
3 Note that the simile is not *throw like a woman*, perhaps because women shouldn't be throwing anything in the first place? That difference would be an interesting one to explore, but I leave it to you to pursue that topic.
4 The popular TV show/YouTube channel *MythBusters* has a wonderful exploration of the physicality of the idea (www.youtube.com/watch?v=LD5Xm5u7UDM or just search for "MythBusters throw like a girl"). There's also an academic article about it – see Robinson et al. (2018).
5 I'm sure lots of you will point out that, for example, men Olympic athletes are in fact faster or stronger than women Olympians. But the problem is that ideologies like the one encapsulated in the phrase *throw like a girl* assume that *all* girls do not throw well, and by extension all women are weaker than all men. This is simply ridiculous. So the "men's records are always better than women's" is a red herring argument that doesn't understand the point. Cameron (2008) is a book-length explanation of such fallacies.

6 This is Zimman's term, which we'll explore more later in this chapter.

7 Ok, 'non-hegemonic' is a pretty obscure way to put it. But I'm not showing off my vocabulary here; I really think this is the best way to put it. We'll see in a bit that there is not only an assumption of heterosexuality when it comes to culture, but also one in which there is a stereotypical script of how men and women come to create desire with one another, and while this script without a doubt differs across cultures and communities, its discovery suggests that there is a 'hegemonic' model of sexuality and desire that structures the way we think about all such relationships, no matter the identities of the people involved.

8 Deborah Cameron has an interesting and typically insightful blog post about this episode; see Cameron (2018).

9 Note that this is not an **acronym**, as LGBTQIA doesn't spell a word.

10 I remind you that categories that are capitalized are done so in order to signal that these are associational groups and not descriptions nor slurs (see Chapter 1).

11 As noted in Chapter 1, I will generally write 'Queer' with a capital 'Q' in order to indicate its use as a categorical descriptor and not a slur; if I'm just talking about the word itself (the **citation form**) I use italics and no capitalization.

12 An excellent audio introduction to the issues around the word *queer* is an episode of the podcast *The Allusionist*: www.theallusionist.org/allusionist/queer. This podcast is about language and linguistics and if you are interested in linguistics you probably want to listen to all of the episodes!

References

Anderson, A. L. H. and Prawat, R. S. (1983). When is a Cup Not a Cup? A Further Examination of Form and Function in Children's Labeling Responses. *Merrill-Palmer Quarterly*, 29(2):375–385.

Bailey, B. H. (2002). *Language, Race, and Negotiation of Identity: A Study of Dominican Americans*. LFB Scholarly Pub, El Paso, TX.

Balhorn, M. (2004). The Rise of Epicene. *They. Journal of English Linguistics*, 32(2):79–104.

Baranowski, M. (2002). Current Usage of the Epicene Pronoun in Written English. *Journal of Sociolinguistics*, 6(3):378–397.

Blackless, M., Charuvastra, A., Derryck, A., Fausto-Sterling, A., Lauzanne, K., and Lee, E. (2000). How Sexually Dimorphic Are We? Review and Synthesis. *American Journal of Human Biology*, 12(2):151–166.

Braun, V. and Kitzinger, C. (2001). "Snatch," "Hole," Or "Honey-pot"? Semantic Categories and the Problem of Nonspecificity in Female Genital Slang. *Journal of Sex Research*, 38(2):146–158.

Cameron, D. (1992). Naming of Parts: Gender, Culture, and Terms for the Penis Among American College Students. *American Speech*, 67(4):367–382.

Cameron, D. (2008). *The Myth of Mars and Venus: Do Men and Women Really Speak Different Languages?* Oxford University Press, New York, NY.

Cameron, D. (2018). Cuntroversy: On Samantha Bee and the C-Word. *Language: A Feminist guide.* https://debuk.wordpress.com/2018/06/03/cuntroversy-on-samantha-bee-and-the-c-word. Accessed June 12, 2018.

Curzan, A. (2003). *Gender Shifts in the History of English.* Cambridge University Press, Cambridge.

Ehrlich, S., Eades, D., and Ainsworth, J. (2016). *Discursive Constructions of Consent in the Legal Process.* Oxford University Press, New York, NY.

Gay and Lesbian Alliance Against Defamation. (2018). Glossary of Terms – Transgender. www.glaad.org/reference/transgender. Accessed September 13, 2018.

Hamilton, M. C. (1988). Using Masculine Generics: Does Generic He Increase Male Bias in the User's Imagery? *Sex Roles*, 19(11–12):785–799.

Hines, C. (1999). Foxy Chicks and Playboy Bunnies: A Case Study in Metaphorical Lexicalization. In Hiraga, M. K. and Wilcox, S., editors, *Cultural, Psychological and Typological Issues in Cognitive Linguistics: Selected papers of the bi-annual ICLA meeting in Albuquerque, July 1995*, pages 9–23. John Benjamins, Philadelphia, PA.

Holland, D. C. and Skinner, D. G. (1987). Prestige and Intimacy: The Cultural Models Behind Americans' Talk About Gender Types. In Holland, D. C. and Quinn, N., editors, *Cultural Models in Language and Thought*, pages 78–111. Cambridge University Press, New York, NY.

Jagose, A. (1996). *Queer Theory: An Introduction.* NYU Press, New York, NY.

Jing-Schmidt, Z. and Peng, X. (2018). The Sluttified Sex: Verbal Misogyny Reflects and Reinforces Gender Order in Wireless China. *Language in Society*, 47:385–408.

Kiesling, S. F. (2002). Playing the Straight Man: Displaying and Maintaining Male Heterosexuality in Discourse. In Cambell-Kibler, K., Podesva, R. J., Roberts, S. J., and Wong, A., editors, *Language and Sexuality*, pages 249–266. CSLI, Stanford, CA.

Kitzinger, C. (2005). "Speaking as a Heterosexual": (How) Does Sexuality Matter for Talk-in-Interaction? *Research on Language & Social Interaction*, 38(3):221–265.

Kulick, D. (2003). No. *Language & Communication*, 23(2):139–151.

Labov, W. (1973). The Boundaries of Words and Their Meaning. In Bailey, C. J. N. and Shuy, R. W., editors, *New ways of Analyzing Variation in English*, vol. 1., pages 340–371. Georgetown University Press, Washington, DC.

Land, V. and Kitzinger, C. (2005). Speaking as a Lesbian: Correcting the Heterosexist Presumption. *Research on Language and Social Interaction*, 38(4):371–416.

Lévi-Strauss, C. (1958). *Antropologie Structurale*. Plon, Paris.

McConnell-Ginet, S. (2006). Why Defining is Seldom 'Just Semantics': Marriage and Marriage. In Birner, B. J. and Ward, G., editors, *Drawing the Boundaries of Meaning: Neo-Gricean Studies in Pragmatics and Semantics in Honor of Laurence R. Horn*, pages 217–240. John Benjamins, New York, NY.

McEnery, T. (2004). *Swearing in English: Bad Language, Purity, and Power from 1586 to the Present*. Routledge, New York, NY.

Newman, M. (1997). *Epicene Pronouns: The Linguistics of a Prescriptive Problem*. Garland, New York, NY.

Preves, S. E. (2002). Sexing the Intersexed: An Analysis of Sociocultural Responses to Intersexuality. *Signs*, 27(2):523–556.

Robinson, L. E., Palmer, K. K., Webster, E. K., Logan, S. W., and Chinn, K. M. (2018). The Effect of Champ on Physical Activity and Lesson Context in Preschoolers: A Feasibility Study. *Research Quarterly for Exercise and Sport*, 89(2):265–271.

Schegloff, E. A. (1997). Whose Text? Whose Context? *Discourse & Society*, 8(2):165–187.

Sidnell, J. (2003). Constructing and Managing Male Exclusivity in Talk-in-Interaction. In Holmes, J. and Meyerhoff, M., editors, *Handbook of Language and Gender*, pages 327–352. Blackwell Publishing Ltd, Oxford.

Stokoe, E. (2006). On Ethnomethodology, Feminism, and the Analysis of Categorial Reference to Gender in Talk-in-Interaction. *The Sociological Review*, 54(3):467–494.

Zimman, L. (2014). The Discursive Construction of Sex: Remaking and Reclaiming the Gendered Body in Talk About Genitals Among Trans Men. In Zimman, L., Davis, J. and Raclaw, J., editors, *Queer Excursions: Retheorizing Binaries in Language, Gender, and Sexuality*, pages 13–34. Oxford University Press, New York, NY.

Zimman, L. (2017). Variability in /s/ Among Transgender Speakers: Evidence for a Socially Grounded Account of Gender and Sibilants. *Linguistics*, 55(5):993–1019.

ction, identity, and performativity

From Lakoff's notion that women use more intensifiers and hedges to the idea that men interrupt women more often, it is in interaction – people talking to other people – that language is most often connected to gender and sexuality. And it is in interaction that people actually experience language. This chapter explores what we know about how gender and sexuality come into play when people are talking to each other. Before we get to gender and sexuality, it's worth exploring how linguists approach studying the patterns that arise in interaction, so I'll start there. Then we look at some of the things that linguists have discovered about how gender relates to turn-taking and interruption, politeness, and indirectness. Next, I turn to ways that address terms (like *sir* and *ma'am*) are used with respect to gender and how speech activities or genres like *gossip* become gendered. Then we'll move to relationships, beginning with the topic of creating sexual desire in interaction, or *flirting*. I'll include a section on homosociality, essentially same-gender friendships, since these have been argued to be even more important than other forms of interaction in how language is structured by gender.

A brief outline of approaches to interactional (discourse) analysis

There's a lot going on when you talk to someone. In fact, one of the reasons it's a bad idea to talk on the phone while driving is that talking actually requires a huge amount of your attention and your brain's processing power. The field of **discourse analysis**, as it is generally called, is thus very broad, so I'll just give you an outline of some of the issues and the ways people look at conversations. This introduction to discourse analysis is not very technical. If you would like a more technical introduction, I recommend the textbooks by Cameron (2001) and Johnstone (2018).

To begin, let's have a look at what you have to do to simply greet someone and have a short conversation about the weather. Let's imagine that this happens, as it often does to me, when you are in an elevator (my office is on the 28th floor of my building, so I spend lots of time riding the elevator). Elevators have their own etiquette: In general, everyone turns the same direction, and that is usually toward the door, giving everyone as much space as possible if you are not riding with friends. Generally, silence is respected, but you might meet an acquaintance on the elevator and thus have time for a one-minute discussion.

Even such a short interaction is a marvel of coordination. The first thing to realize is that neither of you knew you were going to have this conversation until the actual moment it started – you didn't even know you were going to see this person until they got on the elevator with you. But if you think back to all the elevator conversations you've ever had, they generally go pretty smoothly. Sometimes you might think someone is odd, or pushy, or standoffish, but in general, you don't struggle to actually have the conversation. This smoothness is pretty amazing if you think about it, so we must have some general rules or principles in order to manage it. Discourse analysts have found plenty of these, but they don't look like rules in the sense that they tell you what to do. They are more like rules and strategies for a soccer game, which leave it up to the players to take those general rules and actually play the game in response to each other and the semi-random effects of the ball. Just as players have different styles, so do different speakers, and we can analyze how these conversations happen, just like people analyze and dissect soccer games. What we conclude is that having conversations is collaborative in the way playing a sport like soccer is collaborative – you have to work together, even with the other team, to accomplish 'playing a game.' If one side starts using their hands, it's not soccer anymore, and everything falls apart.

Let's put the sports metaphor on hold and return to your elevator conversation. To have this conversation, you first need to get each other's attention and recognize each other's presence. Aside from facial and body language, this will often be accomplished with a greeting and even an **address term**. Let's say their name is Yusif Jones. You could simply say, "Hi Yusif," but then again you may want to make things more formal (or even mock formal, or at least acknowledge Yusif's position) and say, "Hello, Professor Jones." So you've already made a choice about how to say something. (It's a good thing that most of these decisions are relatively automatic or conversations would be very slow.) And if you want to be really casual, you might say "Hey, dude."

At this point, Yusif now needs to recognize you and know what a relevant and preferred response would be. In this case, a greeting follows a greeting. If they remember your name, they might use it. You've now already had a conversation, with two moves. The elevator stops to let someone out, but you don't say goodbye because you don't know them and never talked to them while you were on the elevator. But Yusif says, looking at you, "Is it still pouring out there?" referring to an earlier rainstorm. You have to recognize this utterance as a question, what it refers to, know the answer, and realize that the question means that they have given you the next turn at talk. You respond, appropriately, "Nah, just a drizzle." The two of you have successfully moved the conversation forward; congratulations. You have created an **adjacency pair** with your question and answer, and established a common focus and understanding about the weather.

The conversation could continue with them saying, "Good, I got drenched this morning and I have to go out for lunch." Now, you might think to yourself, "Perhaps they should have brought an umbrella." But you decide not to say that because it wouldn't be polite (later on we will say that such a statement would threaten their **positive face**). They notice that you didn't say anything and realize that maybe that's because you're not prepared to respond with an expression of sympathy or common experience. So before the pause gets too long, they say, "The wind completely destroyed my umbrella." As you say "Oh, that's too bad!" they continue saying something else, but stop with the overlap. You ask them to repeat what they said, and they explain how the umbrella got broken.

So, here you got your signals a little crossed: You thought they were done speaking and they weren't, but you **repaired** the problem and asked them to repeat what they had said. In this way, conversation is not always perfect, but it has mechanisms for fixing itself. Yusif might also interpret your overlap not as an interruption, but as an expression of how involved you are in the conversation.

Now let's imagine that you are a student in Dr. Jones's class. You might say, "So, Dr. Jones, did you happen to get a chance to grade the quizzes yet?" Now you've switched the **frame** of the conversation to talking about the class, and you've asked in a very polite and respectful way (using, as we will call it, **negative politeness**) that displays the power imbalance between the two of you. But Yusif can't resist the power of a question needing to be answered, and grins and says they have finished them and will return them at the next class. You respond, "Thanks, that's great," acknowledging their response and once again showing respect. The door opens and Dr. Jones says, "That's me – Okay, gotta go!" This initiates a whole closing sequence:

YOU: Okay, see you in class!
YUSIF: Yep, bye!
YOU: Bye!

And they walk out the door. As it happens, this is also your stop, but since you've said goodbye, you both walk out as if neither of you are there any longer.

This conversation should seem unremarkable, but there are many things that you and Yusif coordinate with each other, and unspoken messages you give each other, that require a fair amount of work to accomplish. Yet it's not a taxing effort to accomplish, unlike something like a job interview (and another thing you know is that this isn't a job interview, or even part of Yusif's class). You had to take turns and know what turns were appropriate at the time. You had to indicate that you were talking to each other and not the people in the elevator. You had to make contributions that were relevant and polite and friendly. You had to figure out that the other person was also being friendly and polite, and recognize that this would be an instance of 'small talk' and not a deep conversation about the material in the course you are taking.

And that's just a few things that had to happen in this short elevator talk for everything to go smoothly.

So in addition to all that, how does gender and sexuality enter into things? In the last chapter, we saw that the ways we talk sometimes rely on categories that are gendered. That wasn't the case here, but it could have been if, for example, you had been with a friend and then introduced Dr. Jones and said something like "He's my teacher for linguistics." But there may have also been something about Yusif's style that is particularly masculine and you may have been more likely to address them using his title because they are a masculine person.[1] Moving forward in the chapter, we'll explore how gender has entered into many facets of conversation. We'll start with one that recurs over and over and often makes its way into the news: turn-taking and interruptions.

Turn-taking and interruption

There are a lot of popular ideas about gender and interruption, the most common one being that men interrupt women more than the other way around. Popular news stories about this behavior abound and are often the subject of casual comment. This feature of conversation was one of the first to be investigated in the 1970s. The idea that this interruption pattern has to do with the power differences between men and women makes intuitive sense: Men tend to have more power, and women less, so men feel free to simply talk when they want to, even if it means interruption. There is also a stereotype that women are more polite (which I discuss in the next section) and, of course, not interrupting is more polite than interrupting.

So what does the research say? In short, it's mixed, and not as straightforward as one might expect. The earliest studies, such as a study by Zimmerman and West (1975), defined interruption as different from overlapping speech. This difference is very important for research on interruption, where creating an **operational definition** for something that is subjectively felt is one of the main problems. In short, an **overlap** is not always an **interruption**. That is, people overlap speech all the time, partially in anticipation of a turn change that they think is going to happen but doesn't, and partially because some overlaps are meant to signal that we've understood and that the speaker should keep speaking. Sometimes, speakers even finish another speakers' sentence in a cooperative way. But a central defining feature of interruption is that the interrupting speaker is preventing the current speaker from finishing.

So Zimmerman and West defined interruption carefully, suggesting that interruptions only occurred when the overlap couldn't be interpreted in one of the non-interrupting ways. An example of interrupting speech is something like in the following:

A: Yeah, I love going to the beach, we went to the Outer Banks last-
B: Oh cool I love the Outer Banks where did you go?

Here you can see that Speaker A was clearly planning on continuing, as *last* needs a time noun (like *year*) to make any sense (*last year*). It was these kinds of moves that Zimmerman and West defined as interruption.

They found a very strong asymmetry in which men interrupted women much more often than any other gender combination. The problem with this finding is that there were only 20 people in the study and there weren't many conversations. Even Zimmerman and West admit that there aren't enough examples to really generalize that men interrupt more than women (and certainly not beyond a specific class/race/ethnicity/linguistic group), although that's what people tended to do. Following Zimmerman and West, there were more similar studies, and most of them found results that were similar. However, a review of all published studies up to the early 1990s by James and Clarke (1993) found that overall, there was not the evidence to show that this pattern could be generalized. A more recent review of the quantitative literature that took into account a number of factors (Anderson and Leaper 1998) also found little evidence of men interrupting more than women overall. However, when Anderson and Leaper separated out studies that focused only on the clearest and most intrusive interruptions as in the exchange above, they found a significant effect for gender, in which men interrupted more than women, although they do not discuss whether the gender of the person they are interrupting has an effect or not. So the empirical evidence is still not convincing that men interrupt women more than the other way around (although it doesn't really disprove this possibility either).

Yet, many if not most women (at least in English speaking communities) still feel interrupted by men. This feeling could be the prevailing ideology combined with **confirmation bias**. Confirmation bias happens when you notice cases of things that confirm your ideologies and ignore ones that contradict it. For example, if you think that massive doses of vitamin C will cure your cold, then you notice when sniffles go away quickly after taking the vitamin, but you forget the ones where the cold gets worse and drags on (even though studies indicate that vitamin C has only a mild effect on cold symptoms, if any). So, women might remember the times a boorish man interrupted them, but forget about the polite man who didn't, and forget about the boorish woman who did. That is, there may be no gender pattern – it may be that one person was simply boorish – but the person being interrupted may view it through a gender lens.

It may also be true that there is a gender pattern in some more specific way: Another wrinkle in the interruption case is the fact that people interact differently in different situations. So, the same move may feel like an interruption in a high-stakes meeting at work, whereas at a dinner with a few close friends, a similar move may not feel so interruptive. At work, it is important for recognition and promotion to have your ideas heard, whereas it's not as important with your friends and in a casual situation where the goal is just to interact with each other and getting your ideas 'on the record' is less important. Anderson and Leaper found some evidence for this idea in their review, but how the situation can have an effect was problematic and complex and not nearly definitive.

Another challenge for interruption studies is that speakers have varying **conversational styles** which accordingly have different tolerances for interruption. Tannen (1984) introduced this term, and she provides qualitative evidence from a conversation among several friends that some speakers see even the overlap in (1) to be friendly, while others avoid any overlap altogether, including **cooperative overlap** such as words like *yeah* that simply signal the speaker to keep talking. The presence of different styles suggests that even if we can find a pattern of men using more interruptions, we can't necessarily say that the result of the interruption is men dominating conversation or conclude that they were intending to dominate anything (although that could be what is happening). In fact, the opposite could be true – overlap could be friendly. Another example of this kind of high-involvement talk is Schiffrin's (1984) study of "Jewish argument as sociability."

So even if we could objectively say that in similar kinds of situations, or in particular kinds of situations, men use more overlap of a certain kind than women, we couldn't conclude that men are dominating women through interruption. Hilton (2018) supported this view with a carefully constructed experiment that tested perceptions of interruptions among 5,000 American English respondents. She found that Americans who report that they have a more high-involvement style are less likely to find that even a very long overlap is an interruption. Interruptions thus show us the complexity of how gender and interaction work. One person's interruption is another's friendliness, even if it is competitive. Moreover, simply defining interruption is a challenge, and our perceptions can be biased by our gender ideologies and expectations. As we move through some 'gendered' aspects of conversation, we'll see some patterns of use that are more robust but no less affected by these ideologies.

Politeness and indirectness

One of the claims that Lakoff (1975) made was that women were more polite than men because women needed to suppress their individual thoughts and feelings to be 'ladies.' Understanding this claim involves two parts. The first is whether or not women are actually more polite than men, and the second is if they are, then why. As for the first question, there is evidence that on average, women use more politeness than men, at least in European-based societies.[2] As for why, in many ways it seems that Lakoff was on the right track.

In order to explain some of the work in politeness, let's think about what politeness is. I'll explain the main theoretical approach that has been useful in research on politeness. Others have proposed other systems: Lakoff (1973) and Leech (1983) both suggested ways of theorizing politeness by suggesting that there are specific and very general principles such as "Don't impose" and "Give options." However, the dominant theory is that of Brown and Levinson (1987), who take a **strategic** view. That is, they suggest that on some level, we think about what we want to do with an utterance (such as *request, make and assertion, criticize*, etc.), and decide to what extent that is a **face-threatening** move for both us as speakers and for the person we are talking to (we'll explore definitions of **face threats** in a moment).

For example, let's say you are making pizza and I'd like olives on my pizza. So I want to get you to put olives on the pizza. I have to decide what face threats there are to this request. If the face threats are too great, then I might take the strategy of just not making the request at all and have pizza with cheese only. I'd probably do this if I know that your hatred of olives causes nausea simply by my mentioning them, so putting them on your pizza would be a really big ask.

But if you don't have this hatred, I might ask in various ways. I might ask you **directly**, but suggest that I can help chop up the olives, or even fetch them from the store. I might ask you to put olives on the pizza, but I might say how happy it will make me and how grateful I will be. I might ask directly and compliment your pizza making skills. I could also ask **indirectly**, by saying how much I love olives on pizza, or even first asking what you like on pizza and (if you don't say olives) I can say I love olives. Then I would hope you would offer to put olives on. And of course, I might use *please* when asking.

So here's a list of all the ways I've thought about asking for olives:

1   [Don't ask, just sit and hope.]
2   Could you put some olives on the pizza? I can get them out and chop them up if you just tell me where they are.
3   Could you put olives on the pizza? I love your pizza!
4   You make such good pizza, but could please you put olives on? It would be perfect then.
5   You know, I love olives on pizza.
6   What's your favorite pizza topping? I love olives!

Notice that basically all these politeness strategies make it easier to ask something that the addressee might not want to answer positively (except for not doing it, in which case you just stay silent and don't say anything or say something that is not a request). So politeness in this theory is the amelioration of these face threats in conversation. The tricky part of this theory is describing these strategies and understanding **face threats**. Both rely on the notion of **face**, which in this theory is not where your eyes, nose, and mouth are, but "the public self-image that every member wants to claim for [them]self," according to Brown and Levinson (1987). **Face wants** come in two types: positive and negative. **Positive face** is the want of people to be approved of by other people. It's positive because you want to be closer to others (think about positive energy bringing people to you). **Negative face** is the want of people to be left alone and allowed to do want they want (think about negative energy pushing people out of your way so you can get where you want to go). So, the ways of getting olives above can be generalized to different kinds of politeness strategies, as shown below (the first, not doing the act, doesn't really change):

2. Direct ('on record' – you can't deny that you asked for olives), but with a negative politeness strategy. It's negative because I am paying attention to your negative face and building it up. By saying I'll do something for you, I'm asking you to do less, so you can otherwise do what you want.
3. and 4. Direct, with a positive politeness strategy. This is positive politeness because I'm building up your self-worth and image by telling you how much I like your pizza.
5. Indirect, off-record. It's off record because if you respond and say, "sorry, I don't have any olives," I could respond "Oh I didn't mean to put them on, I was just thinking that olives are what I like best."
6. Is a version of 4 and 5, with an indirect request.

Janet Holmes (1995) conducted a number of studies of English speakers in New Zealand, and in general found that women tend to use more positive politeness than men, as well as more **speech acts** that are inherently positively polite, such as compliments (see also Holmes 1988). In addition, she argues that the use of apologies shows that the women in her study offer more apologies and apologize differently than men, or at least for different things. Holmes based her study on observations mainly of students, who noted down apologies they heard as they interacted in their everyday lives. She found an interaction between speaker and addressee gender, such that women apologized to other women almost three times as much as to men, the second highest category. The lowest category was men apologizing to other men. You can see this pattern in Figure 6.1.

However, she also found some interesting gender patterns about the kinds of apologies offered. Women, more than men, tended to provide simple expressions of regret more than men (as in 'I'm sorry'). In addition to those patterns, she found that women's apologies more often served as remedies for space and talk offenses (that is, bumping into people or interrupting) – areas of interaction, Holmes suggests, where women are particularly vulnerable and where they may have developed a greater sensitivity. Men, on the other hand, paid particular attention to time offenses (being late), suggesting that they may have different priorities than women (or, possibly, are late more often than women!). Finally, women used the most apologies to women friends, whereas men apologized most to socially distant women. These findings suggest that apologies may be functioning differently overall for the men and women in Holmes' sample: Women are using apologies to build friendships, while for men it seems that apologies are used to repair more general relationships.

Holmes performed a similar project with compliments, and got similar answers, as shown in Figure 6.2. Holmes, along with some

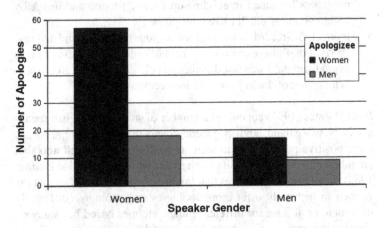

Figure 6.1 Number of apologies by speaker gender and addressee gender. Adapted from Holmes (1995, p. 123).

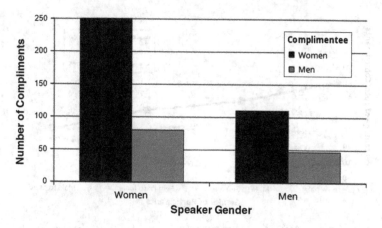

Figure 6.2 Number of compliments by speaker gender and addressee gender. Adapted from Holmes (1995, p. 158).

students, collected compliments heard throughout the day. Once again, there was an interaction between gender of speaker and addressee in the same way as for apologies: Women gave many more compliments to other women than women to men, or men to anyone.

Even more significant was the nature of the compliments, with men more often complimenting the possessions of other men, and women more often complimenting the appearance of other women, as shown in Figure 6.3. These patterns seem to be fitting into ideologies of gender about how men and women are evaluated, with women evaluated on their appearance and men on their possessions and accomplishments.

There are some problems with Holmes' methods, however. First, in all cases, the vast majority of the people collecting the data were women, as were the respondents, so we don't know if the data shows more women giving compliments because they actually compliment more often or simply because the people gathering the data heard more interactions involving women (although they did not have to partici-pate in conversations to hear them – we hear a lot more conversations that we actually take part in!). Similarly, we don't know how many opportunities there were to overhear conversations where compliments could be given. In order to do that, we'd have to know when speakers

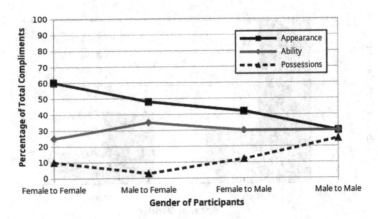

Figure 6.3 Number of compliments by gender and the object of the compliment. Adapted from Holmes (1995, p. 132).

like something enough to potentially give a compliment, which is pretty much impossible.

Women were also found to use politeness differently from men in a place very different from New Zealand. Brown (1980) described the use of politeness markers in the Mexican town of Tenejapa, where the **Tzeltal Mayan** language is spoken. This language has a number of particles which act as **softeners** and **diminutives**, and these particles serve as politeness markers. Brown found that women used many, many more of these particles than men, both when interacting with women and with men. However, she argued that the women used them for positive politeness and support when talking to other women, but to indicate deference when talking to men. Men did neither in most interactions (they show deference when talking to gods, and solidarity when drunk drinking with other men). So here again there are politeness differences, but they are contextualized based on the ideology of gender in that particular culture.

Another important study upends the idea that women are more polite universally. Keenan (1974) described language use in the **Namoizamanga** village in Madagascar, where direct confrontation is discouraged and artful indirectness is seen as a more desirable way to speak than directness (in most European-based societies, especially the

US, directness is more valued). In this community, it is women who are more likely to use direct language and men who are more likely to be indirect. In short, men are more polite by the standards of their use of the Malagasy language.

So what we need is a way to connect the ideologies of gender to those of politeness (which Lakoff suggests in her discussion of why women are more polite, but she doesn't theorize it more broadly). Nevertheless, multiple scholars have criticized the framework of Brown and Levinson, and the quantitative work reviewed above. This criticism follows the change in perspective of language and gender work from the 1980s to the 2000s, and gender theorizing more generally, to focus on how gender makes a difference in particular situations – how linguistic forms are seen as resources for men and women to do things differently, rather than seeing differences in speaking as expressing something inherent about being a woman or being a man. Mills (2003) provided a strong critique that focuses on the generalizations made in these analyses. She argued for a greater focus on the norms created in **communities of practice**, as well as how these communities may reformulate various linguistic forms such as politeness strategies:

> Contrary to Holmes' and Brown's studies, which assert a global difference between men's and women's use of politeness, however mitigated some of their generalisations are, I should like to assert that gender ought not to be seen as a factor which determines the production or interpretation of speech in any simple way … decisions about what is appropriate or not are decided upon strategically within the parameters of the community of practice and within the course of the interaction rather than being decided upon by each individual once and for all.
>
> (2003, pp. 234–235)

What Mills is arguing against here is the idea that politeness strategies are always indexical of gender. While this characterization is a misrepresentation of the research she reviews (which is in general presented as a description of patterns and not interpretation, and which most certainly does not make categorical claims about, for example, women's language vs. men's language), her point that language use is strategic and can be used for interactional goals that are not about gender is an important one. As explained in Chapter 5, this perspective can be captured generally through Ochs's (1992) notion of **indirect indexicality** of gender. Thus, even though the politeness strategies are not strictly (nor explicitly) used to express gender, they may be being used to do things that are more often associated with one gender or another. So even though politeness is not directly indexing gender, it could still be performative of gender if people in certain communities come to recognize or even expect this pattern over and over. There is an interesting interaction with politeness and interruption as well. Recall the recent study by Hilton (2018). In that study, Hilton also found that men who heard a conversation where women were interrupting thought that the women were rude and impolite, but they didn't have this interpretation for interrupting men. This result suggests that there is a connection between the expectation of deference and politeness and gender in the US. Indirect indexicality provides a way to understand the patterning of abstract strategies like the ones described under the idea of politeness and these strategies' relationship to gender ideologies. These connections are even more visible in address terms, which I turn to in the next section.

Gendered address terms

Address terms are words that pick out the person being talked to. They are most obvious when getting someone's attention so that they know you are talking to them. Someone might say to me "Hey Scott!" and I'll look at them and they will begin talking to me directly. Even if I'm listening, I may not be the one addressed, so that I could be listening to two other people talking and then one will turn to me and ask, "So Scott, what do you think?" at which point I am clearly the addressee and I'm supposed to talk. The most generic of these forms is what grammarians call the **second person** (which is *you* in English), and it's a form that you learn early on in any language.

Every language has multiple address term forms, and some actually have multiple second person pronouns. For example, French has the two terms *tu* and *vous*, which both mean *you*. Usually, the difference between them is described as a choice between power (*vous*) and solidarity (*tu*): you use *vous* with someone who has more power than you or you are unfamiliar with, and you use *tu* with people you are closer to, such as friends. In English, there is no such difference in pronouns, but there are differences in terms of address. One of these differences we have already seen in the asymmetry in titles of *Miss, Mrs., Ms.,* and *Mr.* I can be addressed as *Scott, Mr. Kiesling, Dr. Kiesling,* or *sir,* as well as various other names and nicknames. Each one of these suggests a relationship and relevant status, although some more than others: *Scott* doesn't tell me as much about my relationship with a person as *Prof. Kiesling,* the latter of which suggests a student or a colleague (or my boss) addressing me in a formal way.

So address terms tell us a lot about our relationships with the people we are addressing, and those who are addressing us, and since I'm writing about them in this book, you can guess that they are involved in gender. Let's focus on address terms that don't include an actual name in American English: *sir* and *ma'am.* In general, all such address terms are gendered in American English, and they're used generally to address someone you don't know. We talked about these already in the last chapter, since they categorize speakers in particular ways and the person doing the addressing has to know the gender of the addressee (here's where it gets awkward because the system basically makes you choose between *sir* and *ma'am*). Fortunately, in current American English, not using any address term is an option.

There are also many address terms that are used informally and many of these are slang or considered profanity. Even more are developed from terms that were originally insulting. All of these terms tend to do some sort of relationship work. I'm thinking of terms such as *dude, buddy, bro, man* for men and for women terms such as *girl, girlfriend,* and less savory terms such as *bitch* and *slut.* I've done some research on the term *dude* (Kiesling 2004), a term which has expanded in its use over the more than 30 years that I've been using it. *Dude* actually started as an insult to make fun of fancy male dressers, and it eventually had that sense for a particular group of fancy dressers, the *pachucos* gangs in the southwest (as explained by Hill 1994[3]). The men in these gangs turned this insult into a solidarity form of address for each other and it spread from there through various California subcultures such as jazz, beat, hippies, surfers, and skaters. As it spread, it gained meanings and strengthened its connection to masculine speakers before spreading to women in the 2000s. The data in my study was based on interaction in the fraternity I studied, as well as surveys and observations of interactions by language and gender class students in the early 2000s. Since it generally has a masculine meaning, it's not odd that it was used to address men overwhelmingly. But it also was used *by* men more than women, so that using it indexed that the speaker was masculine. In fact, early on, it indexed a particular kind of masculinity, reflecting its path through the California surfing culture.

But it also indexed the relationship between the man who used the term and his addressee. I argued that this relationship was a stance of **cool solidarity**, which was a way of saying "I'm your friend," but in a stand-offish, casual kind of way. The best evidence for this was that in a survey of who they would use it with, respondents almost never reported using dude with someone who was an intimate partner (man or woman). This is a good example of indirect indexicality: In this view, dude indexes cool solidarity in actual interactions, but because cool solidarity is identified with surfer masculinities, it also indexes that group. However, this directionality is probably not how things really work; in reality, the stance and the identity are all wrapped up together and both are indexed at the same time, but the connection between them is important. **Stance** is a term that has variously been defined, but I define it as how a speaker is characterizing their immediate relationship in an interaction. Stance is about our local goals of communicating and the way we represent our ideas and our alignments or 'disalignments' with the people we're talking to.

There is a fascinating parallel here with similar address terms in other languages. In Spanish, especially Mexican Spanish, the term *guey* (pronounced 'way' [wei]) functions in a very similar fashion (see Bucholtz 2009 and an interaction in Kiesling and Johnson 2011). There is also a German form, *alter*, which literally means 'older,' although it is mainly used among young men, primarily from non-German backgrounds. All of these terms are doing interactional work for the men using them to signal their friendly relationships with each other.

So why did women start using *dude*? It seems that they've always used it to some extent, but as the address term began to expand and people heard it in more contexts, its use as a marker of stance was strengthened and its indexing of the speaker as masculine was diminished. A similar path had been taken by the address term *man* in the 1960s and 1970s, to the point that American speakers really don't even notice when a woman uses that term anymore. Similarly, people often ask why women weren't called *dudette*. The answer is partially that it's just longer and more marked than *dude*. But if you know about other address terms in American English, *dudette* just doesn't make sense when there is a term like *girl* or *girlfriend* available. That *dude* expanded to be used by women while terms like *girlfriend* didn't (or at least nearly as much) suggests that there is an underlying unmarkedness to the masculine that women feel comfortable adopting. There is a wide range of other address terms in American English and other languages that I don't have space to include here. But it's worth mentioning that quite a few of them started out, like *dude* did, as insults and not terms of endearment.

But what about terms of endearment such as *honey*, *hon*, *dear*, and *baby*? These are endearments because they are stereotypically used with intimates or children to index an affectionate relationship. However, these terms are sometimes used between people who don't know each other to create a kind of temporary affection, working in a similar way to *dude*. They are rarely used between non-intimate men, but are commonly used from men to women, and women to women. Wolfson and Manes (1979) studied these **endearments** and suggested that they create a stance of caring when used in service encounters and not between true intimates, as if the customer is a child who needs to be taken care of, and that it is women more than men who were addressed in this infantilizing (and patronizing) way.

So both in who is addressed and in the meanings of these terms, interactions in which address terms are used have gender woven throughout. With endearments, there is a possible infantilizing of the addressee. With *dude* used among men, there is an implication of masculine solidarity but also a little homophobia, as endearments are avoided. Men who challenge this dominant heterosexual form of masculinity, then, often use terms such as *girl* or *bitch* to do that work, or to signal what they think about the men they are addressing (usually as part of a community of practice in which they share, but not necessarily). We can see then, that as address terms are used in actual interaction, they can challenge dominant gender ideologies as well as support them.

Gossip

It's not only words and events that can be gendered, but also speech events, speech activities, and genres. In linguistics, **speech events** are abstract templates for events that require speech (which, let's face it, are most events). These templates organize norms about how language is supposed to be used in these events, so that people who share a speech community will have similar expectations about what will happen in the speech event (for example, which **speech acts** are expected), when different people speak, who can participate and how, and what kinds of speech is appropriate. A simple example of this phenomenon is the formal language used in the courtroom, a speech event with specific phases of a trial and kinds of speech, and rules about who gets to speak when and in what way (such as how witnesses have to answer questions in particular ways). Teaching and learning situations – that is, classrooms – also have expectations attached to them, ones that vary from culture to culture (for example, in Korean classrooms, students are authorized to speak much less than in American classrooms). These speech events aren't always in an institutional context; for example, even a family dinner or a serious talk with a friend can have expectations, although they may be less strict. We can group types of events that have similar characteristics (like formal language) into **genres**.

A **speech activity** is similar to a speech event but not connected to a specific event: *lecturing, complaining, joking*, and *cajoling* are examples. We recognize speech activities by the kind of language used and the kinds of things that the speaker tries to accomplish. Such activities are connected to different kinds of speech events but can 'leak' into other speech events. An example is when people I know tell me to stop lecturing in a casual conversation, which sometimes I do because I'm used to lecturing in the classroom, and it sneaks into casual conversation. *Lecturing* is a speech activity which is expected in a class speech event but not in a casual conversation speech event.

Perhaps the most gender-marked speech activity is gossip. **Gossip** is an activity that is closely identified with femininity, to the point that men and women could be doing the same thing but only the women are seen as gossiping. Most definitions of gossip (including the ones that I ask students to write in my classes) are generally focused on speech that is about someone who is not present. Sometimes, the definition includes that what is said about the other person is negative or sala-cious in some way, but not always. The interesting part is that stu-dents, and others I talk to, often suggest that a group of women talking together about *anything* is gossip, as Coates (1988) seemed to suggest. Eckert and McConnell-Ginet (2003) suggested that what is *shoptalk* for men (another speech activity) could be seen as *gossip* for women. Not only is gossip seen as feminine, but it is also seen as frivolous ("Oh, that's just gossip"). This view exists despite the observation that gossip can be a powerful social force, as shown by Harding (1975) for a small Spanish village, in which gossip was used to effectively raise or demolish the status of other villagers.

Several demonstrations show that there is plenty of gossip and gossip-like behavior among men. For example, Cameron (1997) showed how a group of college men discuss another man in their class and criticize his appearance (and speculate about sexuality). In this conversation, they exactly fit most definitions of gossip, but in this particular case, most people don't immediately identify them as gos-siping. Johnson and Finlay (1997) argued that "men's gossip" is about sports and sports figures and analyze a sports talk show to make par-allels between what happens in that show and the definition of gos-sip. Finally, Benwell (2001) showed that the letters pages of men's 'lifestyle magazines' (in which readers write in to magazines that are focused on the activities and concerns of 'being a man') fit definitions of gossip, but that these interactions are rarely discussed as gossip. So even though masculine people do things that fit the formal defini-tion of gossip, it seems that these gossip-y things are less likely to be recognized as such unless there are feminine people involved. So, in some ways, it doesn't matter whether men gossip or not, because the perception is that gossip is feminine.

Is there a masculine-gendered companion to gossip? A recent can-didate is **mansplaining**, a word apparently coined in 2008. The idea behind this term is that someone (usually a man) explains something in a way that communicates that they are absolutely certain and com-pletely knowledgeable about the subject they are expounding upon. The catch is that they are explaining the concept to someone who already knows more about it than they do, or at least as much. For example, if my colleague the physicist confidently explains to me that some languages are better than others, or I confidently explain how faster than light travel is possible to them, then we are mansplaining. 'Mansplaining' is masculine because of the idea that men mansplain more than women (having the morpheme *man* as part of the word of course solidifies this gendering). Given the quick uptake of this term in the US, mansplaining was definitely a speech activity that didn't previously have a name, but it was one that people recognized. Given the connection between masculinity and authoritative stances, it shouldn't be a surprise that people are making a connection between a 'fake' authority and masculinity.

The problem with gendering both gossip and mansplaining is that it tends to essentialize the activity to the gender. So anytime women are talking, their talk is taken to be trivial gossip and any time a man explains something – even if he knows what he's talking about – he is mansplaining. (Which would mean I'd be perceived as mansplaining now, even though in this case I'm pretty sure I know what I'm talking about!) None of this is productive or good for understanding gender and language, but given the gender ideologies underlying these perceptions, it makes sense. That is, masculinity is identified with knowledge and authority, and femininity is identified with 'cattiness' and social machination, and these speech genres are distillations of these gender ideologies in language.

Generalizations about gender and interaction I

So, at this point, what can we say about the interactional styles of masculine and feminine people? I haven't talked about whether men refuse to ask for directions or whether women are talkative (common language and gender stereotypes in the US), although I imagine you can guess that neither of these is proven and that they circulate because of **confirmation bias** – people notice talkative women and generalize from it, but when they notice talkative men, they assign it as an individual trait. And they remember all the times the man didn't ask for directions. One of the themes you'll detect in this chapter and the next, then, is that generalizations about which gender does something more than the 'other' gender are dangerous if not investigated more deeply (and even then, the fact that the question is even posed is part of a gender ideology). For example, if a community attaches politeness to femininity, people in this community are likely to notice women using polite forms more often than they notice men using them. But that's not because the women are actually 'more polite.' Rather, it is because in indexing femininity, politeness helps (or, perhaps, impoliteness hurts). And not all women are going to want to try for the ideal feminine stereotype. The same goes for masculinity: Not all men even try to create what Connell (1995) called **hegemonic masculinity**, but the stereotype nevertheless affects how they act (and speak). So the focus should be on how these ideologies get 'circulated' in communities and cultures, including through language in the ways I explore in this book.

One of the effects of all these stereotypes is to tell people how they *should* be talking, whether to win more friends, win a heterosexual partner, or get a promotion. Cameron (1995) called these sorts of practices **verbal hygiene**. This is another speech activity that is 'gendered,' because most of the advice about how to talk is aimed at women. If you do an internet search for "women should stop saying" you'll find all sorts of lists, most of them aimed at how women should talk in the workplace. Most of the advice suggests turning down the emotional enthusiasm ("not so many exclamation points and emojis!") and turning up the confidence ("don't apologize and don't use the word *just*").[4] But if you search for "men should stop saying," you get, amazingly, some of the same websites as the previous search (about women). When you do find advice for men, it is generally aimed at how not to be boorish at work – to women. The way to find advice for men, apparently, is to search for "how to pick up girls," for which you will find no shortage of advice. The point is that advice about language seems to be overwhelmingly aimed at women (except when organized around developing heterosexual desire in women), even as there is an ideology that women have more verbal ability than men (see Chapter 7). There is no chance that women as a group somehow aren't as good at speaking as men, so this difference must have to do with language once again standing in for something else. In this case, it most likely has to do with the asymmetry of pay and promotion for men and women, and the idea that if women just stopped saying *just* (and perhaps acted more boorishly?), their pay would catch up with men's.

Desire and flirting

Speaking of advice about language, as I just noted briefly, there's lots of advice on the internet aimed at heterosexual men about how to make their voice seductive and cause women to desire them. This observation suggests another speech activity that has not been studied very much in language and gender: **flirting**. Cameron and Kulick (2003) argued that studies of language and sexuality should also include studies of **desire** of many kinds. So one question might be to ask what people do when collaborating to create desire in the *flirting* speech activity. Note that I'm not saying we're studying men verbally *creating* sexual desire in women through interaction; rather, this is about a mutual creation/ display of desire. Questions might include: What do people do and not do with language in order to indicate flirting? What linguistic features trigger a recognition of flirting? How important is 'body language' (more generally called embodiment, which I'll discuss more below)?

Flirting is hard to study, partially because it's not easy to set up situations where you know that flirting will happen. One study tried to discover how this might happen by recording **speed dating** interactions, which take place at an event where one group of people cycles through talking to another one-on-one in short (usually two- to four-minute) interactions, or 'dates.' These are overwhelmingly heterosexual events and after the event is over people have a chance to indicate conversation partners they were attracted to. If the attraction is mutual, contact information is provided. So the whole idea of the interaction is basically to flirt. Korobov (2011, p. 111) studied these interactions and found that "affiliation and compatibility may reflect the extent to which participants are able to create a unique and idiosyncratic connection through coordinated resistance to gender conventionality." This 'resistance' to conventionality was, however, relatively minor, like men saying they are emotional or women talking about being a tomboy. One way to look at this is that there has be a basic level of affiliation and getting along between the two people, but the admission of non-conventionality suggests a vulnerability that creates what appears to be a 'special connection.'

What does this psychologizing suggest for language? I investigated a single interaction between a heterosexual pair that I managed to record while doing research in a fraternity (Kiesling 2013).

The interaction takes place in a bar, with a woman joining a group of men but primarily addressing one man. During the conversation, she indicates that she would like him to stay at the bar longer than he says he can, but also reveals that she was once very drunk at the same bar. It is the last behavior that I argued can be thought of as gender non-conventionality and thus creates a real feeling of flirting. The man also expresses stereotypical aspects of masculine talk, such as unemotionality and a kind of patronizing, paternalistic advice about drinking. So they both play somewhat stereotypical gender roles, except for the transgressive admission by the woman.

I also surveyed students and their friends about whether the interpretation of the conversation described above is flirting depending on the gender of the participants. I created this study by changing the names on the transcript of the interaction to be, for example, two stereotypically men's names or two stereotypically women's names. So the question was, if there were two men saying the same things (or if the genders were 'reversed'), did people still think they were flirting? In fact, there was a significant difference in whether respondents thought the interaction was flirting depending on the gender of the interactants, with the original man-woman pair the most likely to be chosen as flirting, followed by the woman-man pair (the roles reversed), and then the same-gender pairs, with the strongest dispreference for flirting if it was assumed that the two speakers were women. This result shows a definite heterosexual bias in thinking about flirting. In addition, people are more likely to see men as flirting with each other than women. Once again, we see that an interaction is not just stereotyped for gender, but also for sexuality.

Ranganath et al. (2013) also used speed dating data. They used a very large corpus of almost 1,000 'dates' of four minutes which took place in California, and which I assume to be all heterosexual (based on the results; I could not find this explicitly stated). These dates were followed by questionnaires about whether the respondent was flirting and whether they thought the other person was flirting. The researchers then constructed a sample that was coded for a number of linguistic features and trained a computer algorithm to detect flirting. Interestingly, their system overall was better at detecting flirting than the actual humans, mainly because of a bias in humans to think that if they are trying to flirt, the other person is also flirting (humans and their wishful thinking!). The features Ranganath et al. discovered that were predictive of self-reported flirting were different for men and women: "Flirting in women is associated with negation, the word *like*, and collaborative style (appreciations, medial laughter) and ... with the word *I*. Flirting in men is associated with greater use of *you*, *you know*, *um*, and words about sex, as well as less likelihood of talking about work" (p. 111). One of the more interesting features found in this study is the asymmetry of pronoun use, with flirting women more likely to use *I* and flirting men more likely to use *you*. The authors suggest that this indicates that in heterosexual flirting, there is more focus on the woman. I would add that this could be the way that the main direction of desire is supposed to go in romantic scripts in middle-class White American culture, as reported by Holland and Skinner (1987), which I discussed in Chapter 5.

Taken together, all this research suggests that activities that create heterosexual desire are highly organized around stereotypes and are highly variable in their interpretation. That is, flirting is recognized when you are expecting it (or hoping for it). This dynamic can be a powerful motivator for performance and repetition of gender differences: If heterosexual men and women perceive that they will be more successful in attracting partners by using stereotypical interactional styles, then there's a lot of reason to keep using them.

Much of the work described above focuses on face-to-face interaction between heterosexual pairs. However, there has been some interesting research about *online* dating and interaction. For example, Kristine Køhler Mortensen (2017) looks at the interactions of chats between interested heterosexual pairs on a Danish dating website. She finds that one of the most important parts of flirting in this situation is the imagination of a "future shared togetherness." She is interested in the idea that flirting takes place when it is implicit – that is, overt expressions of desire are not useful. But Mortensen finds multiple instances in which couples manage to project activities in the future that are shared, from the immediate, mundane, and probably realizable chat the next day, to a joking reference to a married future with children. Mortensen's work is interesting because it is a more general look at the kinds of discourse moves that people make in creating intimate desire, and does not depend on alignment with dominant ideologies of gender and interaction (you might also be interested in Mortensen's [2015] interesting analysis of women talking about online dating sites, where in effect they talk about desire by committee).

What about homosexual interaction? There is very little work on the creation of homosexual desire in interaction, certainly face to face. However, there have been a number of intriguing directions taken by scholars looking at online dating sites that include homosexual relationships, and some that are exclusively focused on such intimate relationships. One such study is Tommaso Milani's (2013) study of *meetmarket*, a "South African online community for men who are looking for other men." Like some other studies of gay men's online communities (for example, Thorne and Coupland 1998, Boudinette 2017), Milani finds that the self-descriptions tend to highlight traditional or 'straight-acting' masculinities, and the descriptions of the desired other tend to also describe such 'straight-acting' masculinities. To the extent that we might think of these descriptions as creating desire (or flirting), we see that there is a similar tendency, as for the findings of heterosexual flirting, to create desire based on stereotypical identities and romantic scripts. Milani notes, however, that the ways that these men talk about such scripts and identities challenge the ideology that they are in some way innate, or due to the nature of the language user. Rather, they point out the ways in which desire itself is shaped by the language used about desire, as well as the kinds of scripts stereotypically created by these kinds of interactions. For example, one user writes, "I'm not straight acting … I don't act. What you see is what you get!" (Milani 2013, p. 624). This post points to the fact that any way of acting is still 'acting.'

Homosociality and friendship

Another domain of affiliation, closeness, and desire is **homosociality**, which refers to the ways that gender-aligned people create friendships but not romance. In other words, in what way does being of the 'same' gender and being masculine or feminine affect the kinds of interactions you have? Much of the interaction work in language and gender has actually been on this topic, with an underlying assumption that the talk of same-gender groups will allow us to find the differences between those groups. In general, there are many more similarities than differences. But gender ideologies predict different patterns for same-gender friendship interaction for men than for women, especially since overt shows of affection, at least in the European-based cultures that have mostly been studied, is more accepted for women than men (which could also be a reason that the flirting scenario I suggested above is more likely to be seen as flirting for gay men than lesbians).

A focus on same-gender friendship groups has also been the main research topic of the **difference** approach. In two book-length studies of a women's friendship group and some men's friendship groups, Jennifer Coates (1991, 2008, 2013) outlines quite a few characteristics of the particular groups that she studies. In general, she finds that the groups use strategies that align with stereotypes of masculinity and femininity, especially the idea that women have a **collaborative floor** of talking, often offering support and acknowledgement, as well as finishing each other's sentences, while men talk one at a time and tell boastful stories. My characterization of this work is simplifying, but Coates does find differences in the ways that the men's groups and women's groups interact. It is possible that she finds strategies that align with stereotypes of English White middle-class masculinity and femininity because she is looking for them, but it is more likely that the speakers are enacting, through language, those stereotypes to some extent.

The main generalization that Coates, along with Maltz and Borker (1982) and Tannen (1990), makes is that women's talk tends to be more overtly cooperative and supportive and men's talk tends to be more competitive. This is not to say that men are never supportive and cooperative, nor that women are never competitive or mean, but often these relationships are taken up within the cooperative and competitive stances that are gender stereotypes. Penelope Eckert (1989) shows how this can happen for a group of girls. Eckert looks at how competitiveness and cooperation work in one conversation among girls from a high school. She finds that while there is plenty of competition in terms of getting an idea accepted by the group, this competition is done with a cooperative veneer. For example, instead of overt disagreement, arguments are built up through a series of small agreements such that in the end one speaker could carry a consensus of the group.

I found the opposite in some analyses of fraternity talk in which insults were actually seen as friendly (Kiesling 2005). This functioned mostly because it signaled an acceptance by the group. This pattern was no clearer than in an interaction with a prospective member (known as a *rush*, which is also the name for the process of selecting new members), who was set up as a member of the fraternity by suggesting he play softball for their intramural team. The member then metaphorically demoted another member out of the softball batting lineup, but included the prospective member. In this way, the rush was brought into the group and accepted, and desire to be part of the group heightened.

Part of the interaction is shown in Figure 6.4.

In line 1, Saul hails Alex, who is across the room, and in line 2, brings him into a conversation with a question ("What position you gon' play in softball bro?"; *bro* is an address term similar to *dude*, although in 1993 was not used as much as it is today). Given that they are both involved in the fraternity softball team, Saul probably knew that Alex would say 'first base' in response to the question. He then brings the rush into the conversation, and metaphorically the team (and the fraternity) by saying "We have a first baseman right here." What he does next is clever. He turns to the rush and sets up Alex as their 'servant,' who will get water and chewing tobacco (*dip*) for them. He thus performs a desirable friendly insulting relationship with Alex at the same time he brings in the rush to his (dominant)

```
1    Saul:   Hey Alex
2            What position you gon' play in softball bro?
3            (.) ((presumably Alex responds "first base"))
4            Easy now! We got a first baseman right here man!
5            That's all right Alex will get the water for us, in
             between innings?
6    Rush:   ((Laugh))
7    Saul:   We'll have, yknow, in case we need another dip Alex'll
             just pack it up for us?
8            You'll get it packed up for us right Alex?
9    ((Laughter))
10   Rush:   Right get it ready.
```

Figure 6.4 Excerpt from fraternity rush conversation.

side of the insult, and also brings the rush into the fraternity. Keep in mind here that the whole point of the rush process is to create a desire on the rush's part to join the fraternity. This means that what Saul is literally performing is not a negative interaction, but one that feels friendly and positive and calibrated to show what a friendly place the fraternity is.

Marjorie Harness Goodwin's (1990) study focusing on the 'he-said-she-said' activity among a group of Black girls in Philadelphia is also an example of homosocial norms. This activity is one in which a member of the group is called out by saying that someone else said something negative to another member, and that latter member reported it to the accuser. In this case, Goodwin discusses not only how solidarity is built in homosocial groups in a particular community, but also how dispute is accomplished. Indeed, the subtitle of her book is "talk as social organization among Black children," signaling that it is through activities such as he-said-she-said (or the more direct confrontations she finds for the boys) that the social relationships among the children are created and negotiated. The confrontations in the he-said-she-said have consequences for friendship beyond simply 'drama,' and are thus the very stuff of how homosociality is accomplished. (Goodwin also shows how other activities, such as directive use and storytelling, are implicated in this social organization.)

Although much of this research was likely done with the idea that women and men have different styles of interaction, we can also understand the findings in terms of **performativity** and **communities of practice** as discussed in Chapter 4. In this view, the different styles of conversation are not all-encompassing; that is, there is a lot of variety among men and women in how they talk. But we can posit that there is a stereotypical connection of these styles with femininity and masculinity, such that by interacting in these stereotypically gendered ways, men and women are *thinking about* themselves as men and as women, and *desiring to be* (particular kinds of) men and women. In addition, they are interacting *locally*, so that the norms of their community of practice are the immediate focus of their interactions. In the fraternity, joking about subordination was one way of showing acceptance and friendship, and this was done specifically through the topic of sports, which made sense since the fraternity held its intramural success to be central to its identity within the university.[5]

In homosocial interaction, then, we can see the interplay of a local community of practice norms and goals, and more widespread gender stereotypes that nevertheless influence which local norms are pursued. This is an important point for the study of language, gender, and sexuality: There is a balance, or **dialectic** tension, between the immediate experience and goals of a person in a conversation (friendship, recruitment, flirting) and a lifetime of experiences shaped by stereotypes of gender, and of learning and connecting to those stereotypes.[6]

Interaction and embodiment

In recent years, there's been more interest in how language and identity (including gender) are related in people's bodies. For example, researchers have been investigating how gesture and bodily movements add to the meanings created by verbal behavior and how the body might constrain that behavior. So while avoiding **biological determinism** and **essentialism** (the idea that gender differences are innate and biologically determined), we are also interested in how masculine and feminine bodies might affect language, and also whether gender is implicated in the different ways that bodies are recruited by speakers to create a social message. Voigt et al. (2016, p. 678) provide a good definition of **embodiment**: "the complex ways in which the meaning-making capacity of language is tied to the physical bodies of those who use language." The study of how other **semiotic modes** (gesture, head tilt, facial expression, etc.) work with language to create meaning has also been termed **multimodality**, "whereby the production of meaning is always in progress and can recruit resources from diverse semiotic modes including but not necessarily privileging spoken language" (Voigt et al. 2016, p. 678). Studies that focus on either embodiment or multimodality have shown the high degree of integration between language and bodies in interaction and analyses of written and electronic interaction have shown some integration of images and placement of text.

One of the most interesting works in this area is a computer science and linguistics collaboration that uses computer video analysis to match body movements and facial expressions with interactional moves. Voigt et al. (2016) provide an analysis of the **head cant**, in which the head moves down to the side. They note that it is often stereotypically associated with subordination in interaction, and, non-coincidentally, femininity. In data from their lab in which Stanford students interact, and in data from vlogs (video blogs), they find that people in their study associated head cant with linguistic features that index various kinds of alignment to the other person, such as an appeal to shared understanding. But there were also complex ways that it interacted with linguistic features, such that, for example, men were louder when they canted, while when women canted, they showed higher pitch, and used more **discourse markers** such as *y'know* and *I mean*. The results suggest not that body movements that are used in interaction have a direct indexicality to gender, but that they combine with other linguistic resources (such as pitch and word choice), along with other aspects of context, to signal interactional meanings such as stancetaking and turn management. If you recall the multiple functions of interaction from the beginning of the chapter, one way to understand this is that head cant could broadly indicate 'connection,' but that connection can be used for different functions of discourse. For example, the connection could be an appeal to understanding, but it could also indicate a connection such as "I'm listening."

This finding is similar to the function for rising intonation in a Texas sorority found by McLemore (1991). She noted that this intonation, in which statements carry so-called 'question' intonation, was used by the women to simply hold the floor and indicate that there was an upcoming connection to the next statement. But they also used it to show connection to their sorority 'sisters' in the right circumstance, and in some cases, it was heard as 'weak.' So she argued that all these meanings shared the 'unfinished' meaning of the rising intonation (it's unfinished because we expect it to fall at some point – what goes up must come down), and that the intonation draws the listener in. You may have experienced this by feeling you have to respond to a speaker after every utterance that ends in a rising intonation. So the intonation resource was used very differently in specific instances but had a very general overall meaning. The head cant is probably doing something similar, including the meaning of 'connection.' However, both are also associated with femininity, so again we see a connection being made to a more general stance in interaction (connection) and that stance constituting part of the gender identity it is associated with (femininity).

Embodied actions are thus indexed with gender and language in a similar way as other, verbal interactional styles and linguistic forms.

In another study of embodiment, Marjorie Harness Goodwin and H. Samy Alim (2010) showed how a multiracial group of girls at a California school used a particular gesture – the 'neck roll' – to index a "ghetto" identity. But they do this neck roll at the same time as they are using other linguistic means to index a very different "Valley Girl" style. This clash of styles signals that the neck roll is a "mocking transmodal stylization" and does not indicate a wholesale adoption of the identity it indexes ("Ghetto Girl"). Rather, it is used to take a mocking stance of the person the gesture is directed at. The gesture is 'transmodal' rather than 'multimodal' because of the contrast between the gesture and the persona, and it is a 'stylization' because it breaks with the speaker's usual way of interacting. This example is important because it shows how gender is done in the context of creating more particular recognized, gendered identities (that is, "Ghetto Girl" and "Valley Girl"), but not always consistently. Furthermore, these gender stereotypes are used by the girls to take mocking stances toward another girl (in a way that is hard to call out). This shows how the idea of indirect indexicality is also more complex than the original chart shows, as the identities (*Ghetto Girl*) and stances (*mocking*) get connected in ways that draw on the indexicalities of both identity and stance and then get combined in new ways. Most importantly, this example shows how gesture has to be included whenever we do analyses of gender in language in order to fully understand the relationships being constructed and how gender is involved in those relationships. A simple transcript of the interaction would miss the important neck roll gesture that leads to the interpretation of mocking.

Family talk

One of the claims of the so-called 'difference' approach to language and gender (see Chapter 4) is that boys and girls learn different styles of interaction when they are young. Much of this socialization is likely done in the family and with other caretakers in addition to the peer groups studied by researchers such as Goodwin and Eckert. Research on language in the family has borne out this assumption, although the ways that families model and 'police' gendered interactional norms is not always straightforward. First, I'll take a look at some research that complicates an ethnocentric view of language acquisition and then we'll explore a few studies that show how the development of gender stereotypes might be related to family dynamics, especially in White Anglo middle-class, two-parent, two-gender families.

Some of the most interesting studies in this area have been done in the area of language socialization, pioneered by Elinor Ochs and Bambi Schieffelin. Their early work (Ochs and Schieffelin 1995) is focused on two cultures whose interaction with children are very different from European-based societies and middle-class White American culture, with which they contrast the other two. They uncover three very different ways that the cultures relate to both language and how children learn language. The American culture focuses on 'accommodating to the child' in interactions, and the caregivers treat the child as an imaginary interlocutor in interactions. That's why American caregivers use 'baby talk' or 'motherese' when talking to babies and little kids. They also 'speak for' the kids and expand a child's utterance that isn't complete or grammatical (thus helping them talk, so they are accommodating to the kids). The Kaluli of Papua New Guinea are very different. The Kaluli believe that the child does not have language until two specific words are spoken (*breast* and *mother*), and so there is not really any interaction before that, no 'motherese,' and they do not expand a child's utterance. Finally, the Samoan culture does not treat the child as any sort of interlocutor or as an equal. This culture is very hierarchical, meaning that issues of rank and age affect all interactions. Primary caregivers (usually mothers) have other children do many childcare tasks, and once the baby can crawl, they are expected to come to the mother when directed to. There is no baby talk or 'motherese' in Samoa (no, motherese is not universal and biologically programmed!). So learning a language and interaction with mothers is very different in these cultures.

I have simplified Ochs and Schieffelin's wonderfully rich descriptions of family interactions in these cultures considerably and I recommend reading the entire article to understand fully these differences. But the upshot of Ochs and Schieffelin's work is a distinction between cultures in which the caregiver accommodates to the child and those in which the child has to do the accommodating. In White middle-class America, adults accommodate to the child and treat the child as a conversational partner. The Samoans and Kaluli, by contrast, do not accommodate to the child. These differences likely have implications for how society is organized and, to bring it back to gender, how typical caregivers are expected to behave. Since women are the most typical caregivers in all three cultures, the argument goes, White American women are expected to be more accommodating than women in Kaluli or Samoan society. Since these interactions are part of language socialization from day one, they are likely very powerful and deeply felt and contribute to gender stereotypes, even more so when we realize that mothers are often the prototypical woman for young children.

Ochs continued to work on family interactions with an exploration of socialization in American White middle-class interactions, discussed in an article with Carolyn Taylor (Ochs and Taylor 1995). They show how dinnertime activities are asymmetric for fathers and mothers in White, middle-class, two-gender, two-parent households. In the family dinners they studied, all the participants tend to take up different roles when it comes to telling stories at dinnertime. They find that there is a typical situation in which the mother is more often the **introducer** of the story, but the father is more often the **problematizer** for the stories (the person being reported to and asking about the problems), and the father is also the primary recipient of the kids telling the stories. So, for example, a mother will say, "Tell Daddy what happened today," and the kid will tell the story, and then the father will evaluate (for example, praising the child for an accomplishment). In this way, various gendered roles are again reinforced, and in this asymmetry, we see the woman doing the work to facilitate the interaction, while the men judge the action. Ochs and Taylor also found evidence that similar dynamics happen when it is the mother or father telling the story. Ochs and Taylor call this the "Father Knows Best" dynamic, after a 1950s TV sitcom of the same name. Not only does this dynamic show an asymmetry for the current differently gendered parents, but it also models gendered interaction for the kids, who learn that men and women play different roles in interaction.

Shari Kendall (2008) finds similar evidence as Ochs and Taylor but looks at all family conversation and not just narratives. She approaches the question from a framing analysis, so let me explain a bit about what such an analysis is. An **interactional frame** is an abstract idea of 'what is going on' in interaction. We need to know what a frame is in order to interpret any interaction appropriately. For example, you probably don't usually come into a classroom and immediately start having class. Rather, there's a period before class in which you talk to other students or ignore the teacher or both, even though you are all in the room together. Then the teacher signals the beginning of class. Nothing has physically changed but saying something to your neighbor now has a different meaning than it did before the teacher changed the frame. Even within the class time, there might be a 'group work' frame and a 'lecture' frame, for example, and people play different roles in different frames.

Kendall used this idea to look at family conversations. She found a difference in how members of one family interact. While the data are only for one family, the results are similar to Ochs and Taylor's, and align with White, middle-class American gender ideologies. Kendall finds 15 different kinds of positions within 5 main frames. The frames are *Dinner*, *Caregiving*, *Socialization*, *Managerial*, and *Conversation*. She finds that the mother does most of the talking, and that the father has minimal roles in most frames. He is most present in *conversation*, where he takes up a 'journalist' and 'comedian' position. Kendall shows how these roles play out in actual interactions, as the father takes a 'director' and mostly playful roles with the kids. While this is only one family, this asymmetry shows more support for the idea that family interaction can affect how kids learn about gender and gendered ways of speaking. Taken together, these studies show that the family is an important site of socialization for interaction, and moreover that it is one in which gender is often highlighted, given the typicality and ideology of having a two-parent (of different genders) family.

Generalizations about gender and interaction II

All of the examples we have seen so far in this chapter move the analysis of gender in interaction away from a search for differences between gender to a more complex and subtle view that shows an interaction of other social roles and stances with gender. To put it very simply, people never just stand up and utter a string of words in a way in order to sound masculine or feminine; rather, they are engaged in doing other things in interaction, such as the various dinnertime positions just discussed, or creating or displaying desire. In these views of gender and interaction, even the notion of indirect indexicality looks simplistic, because different ways of talking and different forms used in interaction create not a single meaning but a host of interconnected possible meanings depending on the previous contexts of use. This complexity and lack of certainty can get frustrating, I know. But the beauty of human interaction is in its creativity, subtlety, and contingency. If it were simple, it would be boring.

A particularly salient example comes from Michael Furman's (2018) analysis of *mat* (which is basically Russian for *swear words*) among punk women in Saint Petersburg, Russia. Furman notes that in Russian mainstream society, there is a strong taboo against women swearing and that *mat* is heard as masculine by most Russians. In his ethnography of punk culture in Saint Petersburg, Furman finds punk women swear a lot (at one point commenting that he heard more *mat* in listening to one of the women for 15 seconds than in 12 months working at a mainstream organization). He suggests that at first it may be tempting to think that punk women are simply 'more masculine.' But he argues that, even though the *mat* retains a connection to masculinity, the women's use of *mat* is more complicated than that, and the meanings more limited to the particular interaction and community of practice (punks). For example, in one example, one of his participants, Lena, is simply expressing her amazement at the abundance of wild strawberries she and her group have found (Furman 2018, p. 17), but she uses abundant *mat*: "Lena's consistent use of *mat* while gathering strawberries transforms a passive, feminine activity (picking strawberries) into an active performance of masculinity. Indeed, strawberries abounded to such an extent that Lena remarked that she is 'up to [the] cock' in strawberries. While strawberries themselves do not carry social gender, Lena's description of the strawberries as 'up to cock' does." But there's more than just gender going on in this situation. *Mat* is a resource to do interactional work that has other value in this community of practice and creates *authoritative* stances. Indeed, one of Furman's main points is that the use of *mat* is mainly for stancetaking (creating authority) and these stances are (not coincidentally) simultaneously connected to masculinity – another example of indirect indexicality. The effects in the strawberry example are multiple: Lena creates an authoritative interactional stance that aligns with another member of the group, creates solidarity between them, and shows her membership in the punk community. So *mat* is used for 'practical' (immediate) interactional purposes and meanings, but the link with masculinity is still there, and arguably part of the reason why it is connected to the punk subculture in the first place.

So we can look at linguistic forms such as *mat* as resources that have a bundle of potential meanings and those will be affected by all the things going on at the time and being done by the speaker in a community with its own set of meanings. Gender comes into this complex picture in two ways. It is a salient social category that people notice and is thus attached to forms directly, and also to other social categories. But the importance of gender changes depending on the community and the interaction within that community. In the Russian case, *mat* changes its meaning depending on whether it is uttered by a woman or a man, and whether that woman or man is in the punk community. Gender makes a difference, even if using *mat* doesn't simply mark one as 'being a man.'

Rape and consent

In the previous chapter, I discussed some of the ways the categorizing power of language affects how we think about what constitutes *rape*, and how that affects how we think about sex and power. Since in this chapter we are talking about interaction, it's important to think about how interaction can affect how people think about the idea of **sexual consent**. While research has not focused much on the actual consent interaction (it's not easy to get ethical recordings of those), there has been considerable study of the disputes that occur when one party argues that consent was not given – in other words, **rape** (although many victims do not even think of it as rape, given the ways rape is stereotypically thought of as a violent attack by an unknown man). This is a subject of powerful emotion, with some on one side believing that rapists (usually men) are inappropriately punished, while on the other side, many argue that sex without consent happens much more frequently than thought. The fact is that most non-consensual heterosexual sex happens between people who know each other and have often started a romantic encounter. In the context of this chapter, we are concerned with the ways in which ideologies about gendered interaction and what are called **language ideologies** affect both consent and the adjudication of encounters as rape. Language ideologies are ways that people think about how language works. In this case, the relevant language ideology is one that understands all the meanings of an interaction to arise simply from the words in a single utterance, rather than appreciating that the context of the situation can change the meaning. This view means that if someone utters words that give consent, no matter the fear or implied coercion present, consent has been given.

Susan Ehrlich is a linguist who has worked extensively on both the construction of consent and especially the ways that consent is discussed and challenged in judicial settings (see Ehrlich 1998, 2001, 2012). Over the last two decades, her in-depth analyses of judicial situations show how gender and language ideologies interact in the construction of consent, or in these cases, in judgements about whether consent was given. The first case (Ehrlich 1998) involves a university tribunal in which a man was accused of having sex with two different women without their consent. The tribunal was not an official government trial but a hearing in the university in which the participants were students. Ehrlich focuses mainly on the interaction with one woman. Essentially, the woman allowed the man to come to her dorm room and get in bed with her, where they had sex. She says she never gave consent and he said that there were ways in which he inferred consent. The main problem with the encounter was the idea that the woman had to very explicitly say *no* to the sexual advances at some point, as opposed to the idea that the man should have asked unequivocally whether they could have sex.

Ehrlich shows that not only the man but the 'judges' of the tribunal had an ideology in which women and men do not communicate well (see the 'difference' explanation for language and gender differences in Chapter 5). Moreover, this 'miscommunication' was the woman's responsibility. In this case, we see not only a gender ideology but also a language and gender ideology at work, in which people's assumptions about language and gender affect how they understand interactions. In addition, there is an ideology that the woman must say *no*, otherwise consent is given. Finally, there is an ideology of interaction in which context and power is not taken into account, in which it does not matter that a larger and more powerful person is in the room, making it more difficult to say *no*. This facet of the situation did not seem important to the tribunal members. This ideology of language – that meaning always resides in the words spoken and not in other modes or in the situation at hand – is common in European-based societies and especially in legal contexts.

One of the important ideas in Ehrlich's work is the idea that pieces of language are taken from one context and used in another. To put some terminology to this, they are both **entextualized** and **recontextualized**. Entextualization is the notion that bits of language become thought of as a single 'chunk' that can then be transported to other contexts. You can see this all the time with quotes that get repeated; an extreme form is the idea of the internet 'meme' (which often also includes pictures or video, but the idea is the same), in which a piece of interaction or language becomes reified and so can be used in other situations. These 'other situations' are recontextualizations of the original 'text,' and because of the new context are interpreted slightly differently, but with an 'echo' of the original. These ideas are important in the judicial setting, in which much of what goes on is to interpret past events and then put them into a category that makes them criminal or not, and those past events are more often than not speech events.

In another article, Ehrlich (2012) uses these ideas to show how they are applied in a trial in a case of 'post-penetration rape,' a situation in which consent is given but then withdrawn after intercourse begins. In the case Ehrlich analyzes, two men raped a woman in the back of a car in a parking lot. The first man rapes her without consent (this fact is not under dispute), and then the other man asks, "Will you let me take my turn?" to which she replies, "Will you stop when I say stop?" As Ehrlich points out, this kind of assent can be a defense mechanism for the woman to avoid harm or death and it is certainly not perceived by the woman as freely given in the circumstance. But in the trial, the circumstances of this exchange are stripped away, so that the woman's question ("Will you stop when I say stop?") becomes entextualized and used by the defense to argue that for the second man, consent was given. As Ehrlich says, "a context-free reading of Jewel's qualified agreement eliminated the series of non-consensual sexual acts that preceded it and, thereby, made difficult its interpretation as coerced agreement, that is, as submission or compliance motivated by a fear of more prolonged or extreme instances of violence" (Ehrlich 2012, p. 59).

So here again we see important ways in which how people think about language and interaction affect how they see 'what happened,' with huge consequences for justice. Interactional patterns and ideologies are therefore important to gender not just in understanding differences or seeing the effects of gender ideology, but understanding the effects of gender ideology on the interpretation of talk in high-stakes interactions like sexual encounters and trials. Even without the patterns described previously, the idea that masculine voices are more likely to be associated with authority makes the construction of authority in trials (or the workplace or elections) to be more difficult for women. In the case of the trials as well, we see ideologies of gender and desire at play in the interpretation of the women's talk, in which they are interpreted as being responsible for saying *no* more than men are responsible for asking the question in the first place.

Gender in new media

While most interactions we've looked at in this chapter are oral and mostly face to face, much interaction in our era takes place using screens and keyboards. These electronic interactions have caught the eye of researchers wondering to what extent gender enters into the way people use these newer ways of interacting. In general, the forces that work 'in real life' (IRL) also work in computer-mediated discourse (CMD), as Susan Herring and Jannis Androutsopoulos (2015) call it. So, simplistically, is there a difference in how men and women use language on the internet (alternately, what difference does someone's gender make for interaction online)? However, within CMD studies, there are many other more specific questions, such as what **mode** is used by different genders (text, chat, comments on sites like YouTube, Facebook, Twitter, Instagram, Snapchat, and no doubt something new that will have appeared recently) and how? Finally, there's a tension between the democratizing way that some interactions on the internet can strip away and complicate gender and identity, and the way that the CMD has many gatekeeping functions that shape the way people experience it, including by gender.

So the first thing we might ask is similar to the approaches to gender and interaction taken early in the study of language and gender: Does gender predict a difference in the use of specific linguistic features? In general, there are findings that there are some 'gendered' styles, although these are difficult to test because it is not always possible to find out the gender of the participant in CMD. So, in interaction that is anonymous, we really don't know if men and women participate differently. There are some claims that similar interactional features occur in online spaces that are '**nonymous**' (in which people are identified, the opposite of *a*nonymous), such as women using more emoticons and emoji (see Witmar and Katzman 1997, Wolf 2000, and the review in Herring and Stoerger 2014). The question of what mode and platform people use is a fast-moving target. Facebook was started in 2004, and really took off in 2008 (Wikipedia 2018). But in general, there seem to be some asymmetries by gender, for example, with women using sites such as Facebook and Twitter slightly but consistently more than men (Pew Research Center 2018). In addition, there is differential use of mobile (that is, smartphone, tablet, etc.) interface usage and usage from laptop and desktop computers, and how mobile devices are used (it seems that women use them for more social interaction, men for information seeking; see Herring and Toerger 2014, p. 575). These gender patterns no doubt intersect with other social categories such as age, class, race, nationality, and so on, making any generalizations about gender extremely problematic. Research in the future, it seems, looks to follow the model of language and gender and see gender as one piece of the complex identities that people create online, as people mix in different ways of being feminine, masculine, or neither into their online identities.

So CMD is an extremely fast-moving and otherwise difficult set of language usages for researchers to understand. And, as you may have noticed as you read through this book, researchers have become less and less interested in whether there are statistical differences in language use in interaction with a binary gender model.

But gender *is* relevant to many interactants online, as is especially evident in situations of gender gatekeeping (and other sorts of gatekeeping). Lauren Collister (2016) provides an analysis of how this gatekeeping works, beyond more sensational stories of harassment and insult such as 'Gamergate' (Dewey 2014) and general harassment (for example, of Kelly Marie Tran; see Clark 2018). Collister describes a situation in which she is playing the game *World of Warcraft* but decides not to engage in voice chat (in which people talk in the 'real' voices) in order to keep her femininity hidden, based on previous harassment in the past. In this way, we see that harassment, insults, and even not taking women seriously has serious gatekeeping effects. (Note also that the fact that the vast majority of the internet and games are in English privileges those who are native speakers of English as well.)

Notes

1 You will have noticed that I used the pronoun 'they/them' throughout most of the examples when referring to Yusif Jones. This was intentional, even though for many people 'Yusif' is heard as masculine. Does the non-gendered pronoun make a difference? How so?

2 I use the term 'European-based' for a few reasons. I don't find any of the categorizations such as 'developing' or 'third world' or 'West' (west of what? Is Africa West?) to be very descriptively accurate. I am not strictly talking about Europe, but also many countries that were once colonies, such the US and New Zealand. Even then, I'm not really talking about all of the US or New Zealand. And I'm not talking about all colonies either. So it's basically cultures that are closely related to White (still problematic) European societies (and probably northern ones at that). Categories like this always leave something out, so there are still problems, but you get the idea!

3 Although Hill's claims about the origins of the word have been proved wrong; the term originated as a shortening of 'Yankee Doodle Dandy,' where a *dandy* is a sharp dresser. See www.chronicle.com/blogs/lingua-franca/2013/10/21/dude.

4 https://jezebel.com/google-exec-women-stop-saying-just-so-much-you-sound-1715228159; www.annawickham.com/6-things-women-should-stop-saying-at-work.

5 Sports competition among different groups within a single university, as opposed to intermural sports in which teams from different universities compete against one another.

6 **Dialectic** technically refers to a mode of philosophy and argument in which a clash of opposites reveal a truth (put relatively simplistically). It is often used, as here, to refer to situations in which there are two somewhat opposing forces or influences but neither is primary, and their interaction and pull create the situation being described.

References

Anderson, K. J. and Leaper, C. (1998). Meta-Analyses of Gender Effects on Conversational Interruption: Who, What, When, Where, and How. *Sex Roles*, 39(3–4):225–252.

Baudinette, T. (2017). Constructing Identities on a Japanese Gay Dating Site. *Journal of Language and Sexuality*, 6(2):232–261.

Benwell, B. (2001). Male Gossip and Language Play in the Letters Pages of Men's Lifestyle Magazines. *The Journal of Popular Culture*, 34(4):19–33.

Brown, P. (1980). How and Why are Women More Polite: Some Evidence from a Mayan Community. In McConnell-Ginet, S., Borker, R., and Furman, N., editors, *Women and Language in Literature and Society*, pages 111–136. Praeger, New York, NY.

Brown, P. and Levinson, S. (1987). *Politeness: Some Universals in Language Usage*. Cambridge University Press, New York, NY.

Bucholtz, M. (2009). From Stance to Style. In Jaffe, A., editor, *Stance: Sociolinguistic Perspectives*, pages 146–170. Oxford University Press, New York, NY.

Cameron, D. (1995). *Verbal Hygiene*. Routledge, New York, NY.

Cameron, D. (1997). Performing Gender Identity: Young Men's Talk and the Construction of Heterosexual Masculinity. In Johnson, S. and Meinhof, U., editors, *Language and Masculinity*, pages 47–64. Blackwell, Malden, MA.

Cameron, D. (2001). *Working with Spoken Discourse*. Sage Publications, London; Thousand Oaks, CA.

Cameron, D. and Kulick, D. (2003). *Language and Sexuality*. Cambridge University Press, New York, NY.

Clark, T. (2018, June 5). 'Star Wars: The Last Jedi' actress Kelly Marie Tran deleted all her Instagram posts after months of harassment. *Business Insider*. www.businessinsider.com/star-wars-actress-kelly-marie-tran-deletes-instagram-posts-after-harassment-2018-6. Accessed June 18, 2018.

Coates, J. (1988). Gossip Revisited: Language in All-Female Groups. In Coates, J. and Cameron, D., editors, *Women in Their Speech Communities: New Perspectives on Language and Sex*, pages 94–122. Longman, London.

Coates, J. (1991). *Women Talk: Conversation Between Women Friends*. Blackwell, Malden, MA.

Coates, J. (2008). *Men Talk: Stories in the Making of Masculinities*. Blackwell, Malden, MA.

Coates, J. (2013). *Women, Men and Everyday Talk*. Palgrave Macmillan, New York, NY.

Collister, L. B. (2016). "At Least I'm Not Chinese, Gay, or Female": Marginalized Voices in *World of Warcraft*. In Squires, L., editor, *English in Computer-Mediated Communication: Variation, Representation, and Change*, pages 351–376. De Gruyter Mouton, Boston, MA.

Connell, R. W. (1995). *Masculinties*. Polity Press, Cambridge.

Dewey, C. (2014, October 14). The only guide to Gamergate you will ever need to read. *The Washington Post*. www.washingtonpost.com/news/the-intersect/wp/2014/10/14/the-only-guide-to-gamergate-you-will-ever-need-to-read. Accessed June 18, 2018.

Eckert, P. (1993). Cooperative Competition in Adolescent 'Girl Talk'. In Tannen, D. editor, *Gender and Conversational Interaction*, pages 32–61. Oxford University Press, New York, NY.

Eckert, P. and McConnell-Ginet, S. (2003). *Language and Gender*. Cambridge University Press, Cambridge; New York, NY.

Ehrlich, S. (1998). The Discursive Reconstruction of Sexual Consent. *Discourse & Society*, 9(2):149–171.

Ehrlich, S. (2001). *Representing Rape: Language and Sexual Consent*. Sage, New York, NY.

Ehrlich, S. (2012). Text Trajectories, Legal Discourse and Gendered Inequalities. *Applied Linguistics Review*, 3(1):47–73.

Furman, M. (2018). Of Mat and Men: Taboo Words and the Language of Russian Female Punks. *Laboratorium*, 10(1):5–28.

Goodwin, M. H. (1990). *He-Said-She-Said: Talk as Social Organization Among Black Children*. Indiana University Press, Bloomington, IN.

Goodwin, M. H. and Alim, H. S. (2010). "Whatever (Neck Roll, Eye Roll, Teeth Suck)": The Situated Coproduction of Social Categories and Identities Through Stancetaking and Transmodal Stylization. *Journal of Linguistic Anthropology*, 20(1):179–194.

Harding, S. (1975). Women and Words in a Spanish Village. In Reiter, R., editor, *Toward an Anthropology of Women*, pages 238–308. Monthly Review Press, New York, NY.

Herring, S. C. and Androutsopoulos, J. (2015). Computer-Mediated Discourse 2.0. In Tannen, D., Hamilton, H. E., and Schiffrin, D., editors, *The Handbook of Discourse Analysis*, 2nd Edition, pages 127–151. Wiley, Malden, MA.

Herring, S. C. and Stoerger, S. (2014). Gender and (a)nonymity in Computer-Mediated Communication. In Ehrlich, S., Meyerhoff, M., and Holmes, J., editors, *The Handbook of Language, Gender, and Sexuality*, 2nd edition, pages 567–586. Wiley, Malden, MA.

Hilton, K. (2018). What Does an Interruption Sound Like? Doctoral Thesis, Stanford University, Department of Linguistics. Viewed December 13, 2018, purl.stanford.edu/vf660gm5432.

Holland, D. C. and Skinner, D. G. (1987). Prestige and Intimacy: The Cultural Models Behind Americans' Talk about Gender Types. In Holland, D. C. and Quinn, N., editors, *Cultural Models in Language and Thought*, pages 78–111. Cambridge University Press, Cambridge.

Holmes, J. (1988). Paying Compliments: A Sex-Preferential Politeness Strategy. *Journal of Pragmatics*, 12:445–465.

Holmes, J. (1995). *Women, Men and Politeness*. Longman, London.

James, D. and Clarke, S. (1993). Women, Men, and Interruptions. In Tannen, D., editor, *Gender and Conversational Interaction*, pages 231–280. Oxford University Press, Oxford; New York, NY.

Johnson, S. and Finlay, F. (1997). Do Men Gossip? An Analysis of Football Talk on Television. In Johnson, S. and Meinhof, U., editors, *Language and Masculinity*, pages 130–143. Blackwell, Malden, MA.

Johnstone, B. (2018). *Discourse Analysis*, 3rd Edition. Blackwell, Malden, MA.

Keenan, E. (1974). Norm-Makers, Norm-Breakers: Uses of Speech by Men and Women in a Malagasy Community. In Bauman, R. and Sherzer, J., editors, *Explorations in the Ethnography of Speaking*, pages 125–143. Cambridge University Press, Cambridge.

Kendall, S. (2008). The Balancing Act: Framing Gendered Parental Identities at Dinnertime. *Language in Society*, 37:539–568.

Kiesling, S. F. (2004). Dude. *American Speech*, 79(3):281–305.

Kiesling, S. F. (2005). Homosocial Desire in Men's Talk: Balancing and Re-Creating Cultural Discourses of Masculinity. *Language in Society*, 34:695–726.

Kiesling, S. F. (2013). Flirting and 'Normative' Sexualities. *Journal of Language and Sexuality*, 2(1):101–121.

Kiesling, S. F., and Ghosh Johnson, E. (2010). Four Forms of Interactional Indirection. *Journal of Pragmatics*, 42(2):292–306.

Korobov, N. (2011). Gendering Desire in Speed-Dating Interactions. *Discourse Studies*, 13(4):461–485.

Lakoff, R. T. (1973). The Logic of Politeness; or, Minding Your P's and Q's. In C. Corum, C., Cedric Smith-Stark, T., and Weiser, A., editors, *Papers from the Ninth Regional Meeting of the Chicago Linguistics Society*, pages 292–305. Department of Linguistics, University of Chicago, Chicago, IL.

Lakoff, R. T. (1975). *Language and Woman's Place*. Harper & Row, New York, NY.

Leech, G. (1983). *Principles of Pragmatics*. Longman, London; New York, NY.

Maltz, D. and Borker, R. (1982). A Cultural Approach to Male-Female Miscommunication. In Gumperz, J. J., editor, *Language and Social Identity*, pages 196–216. Cambridge University Press, Cambridge.

McLemore, C. A. (1991). *The Pragmatic Interpretation of English Intonation: Sorority Speech*. PhD thesis, University of Texas at Austin.

Milani, T. M. (2013). Are "Queers" Really "Queer"? Language, Identity and Same-Sex Desire in a South African Online Community. *Discourse & Society*, 24:615–633.

Mills, S. (2003). *Gender and Politeness*. Cambridge University Press, Cambridge.

Mortensen, K. K. (2015). A Bit Too Skinny for Me: Women's Homosocial Constructions of Heterosexual Desire in Online Dating. *Gender and Language*, 9(3):461–488.

Mortensen, K. K. (2017). Flirting in Online Dating: Giving Empirical Grounds to Flirtatious Implicitness. *Discourse Studies*, 19(5):581–597.

Ochs, E. (1992). Indexing Gender. In Duranti, A. and Goodwin, C., editors, *Rethinking Context*, pages 335–358. Cambridge University Press, New York, NY.

Ochs, E. and Schieffelin, B. (1995). Language Acquisition and Socialization: Three Developmental Stories and Their Implications. In Blount, B. G., editor, *Language, Culture, and Society*, pages 470–512. Waveland Press, Prospect Heights, IL.

Ochs, E. and Taylor, C. (1995). The "Father Knows Best" Dynamic in Dinnertime Narratives. In Hall, K. and Bucholtz, M., editors, *Gender Articulated: Language and the Socially Constructed Self*, pages 99–122. Routledge, New York, NY.

Pew Research Center. (2018). Social media fact sheet. www.pewinternet.org/fact-sheet/social-media. Accessed June 3, 2018.

Ranganath, R., Jurafsky, D., and McFarland, D. (2013). Detecting Friendly, Flirtatious, Awkward, and Assertive Speech in Speed-Dates. *Computer Speech & Language*, 27(1):89–115.

Schiffrin, D. (1984). Jewish Argument as Sociability. *Language in Society*, 13(3):311–335.

Tannen, D. (1984). *Conversational Style: Analyzing Talk Among Friends*. Ablex, New York, NY.

Tannen, D. (1990). *You Don't Just Understand: Women and Men in Conversation*. William Morrow and Co., New York, NY.

Thorne, Adrian, Coupland, Justine. 1998. Articulations of Same-Sex Desire: Lesbian and Gay Male Dating. *Journal of Sociolinguistics*, 2(2):233–257.

Voigt, R., Eckert, P., Jurafsky, D., and Podesva, R. J. (2016). Cans and Cants: Computational Potentials for Multimodality with a Case Study. *Journal of Sociolinguistics*, 20(5):677–711.

Wikipedia. (2018). Facebook. https://en.wikipedia.org/wiki/Facebook#User_growth. Accessed June 3, 2018.

Witmer, D. and Katzman, S. L. (1997). On-Line Smiles: Does Gender Make a Difference in the Use of Graphic Accents? *Journal of Computer-Mediated Communication*, 2(4). http:// onlinelibrary.wiley.com/doi/10.1111 /j.1083-6101.1997.tb00192.x/full.

Wolf, A. (2000). Emotional Expression Online: Gender Differences in Emoticon Use. *Cyber Psychology & Behavior*, 3:827–833.

Wolfson, N. and Manes, J. (1979). Don't Dear Me. *Working Papers in Sociolinguistics*, No. 53. ERIC Clearinghouse, Washington, DC.

Zimmerman, D. H. and West, C. (1975). Sex Roles, Interruptions and Silences in Conversation. In Thorne, B. and Henley, N., editors, *Language and Sex: Difference and Dominance*, pages 105–129. Newbury House, Rowley, MA.

Chapter 7

Linguistic norms as gender norms

Linguistic variation and change: A short introduction

This chapter's title suggests a connection between linguistic and gender 'norms.' This may strike you as a bit odd, since it seems that we've been discussing both gender norms and linguistic norms for the entire book. But in this chapter, we approach things a bit differently, following a linguistic subfield known as **linguistic variation and change**, sometimes also referred to as **sociolinguistic variation**. So we're going to get into the details of linguistic systems as well as why and how languages change (naturally, gender plays into these hows and whys). I'll start by explaining a bit about how the study of variation is conceived and then, in the next section, we'll bring in gender explicitly and how it has been important for this subfield. At the end of the chapter, I'll suggest some of the ways this approach to studying gender and language can be connected to categorization and interactional approaches.

Sociolinguistic variation arose out of another subfield of linguistics: historical linguistics. Historical linguistics predates the modern linguistics that developed in the last century, and in many ways is the forerunner of all modern 'Western' linguistics. In the 19th century, a few smart Europeans noticed that there were similarities among words across several languages, and posited that those similarities must exist because the languages are somehow 'related,' much in the way people with similar ancestors have similar physical traits. The eventual outcome of this observation was the categorization of languages in different language 'families,' so that, for example, English and German are both in the Germanic language family, which itself belongs to a very large family called Indo-European (Campbell [2013] is a good introduction to this field.).

So, historical linguists compare languages and deduce what kinds of changes must have happened in the different languages and reconstruct their language ancestors. Based on these patterns, they have developed general principles that suggest how and why languages change. Historical linguistics is one of the oldest subfields of linguistics (beginning in the 18th century), and until recently, researchers in this subfield always looked at changes *after* they were finished, because they thought they couldn't see changes as they actually happened. But in the 20th century, scholars began to wonder if they could observe a change as it was in progress. In the early part of the century there were a few attempts, but the recording of such changes was difficult until technology made it possible to record and measure language easily (equipment that, by today's standards, was clunky and huge, but at least it was possible).

The beginning of the subfield is generally traced to William Labov's study of changes in vowel pronunciation on the island of Martha's Vineyard off the northeast coast of the US in Massachusetts (Labov 1963). Labov developed techniques to interview Vineyarders on audiotape, measured some of their speech, and then compared how speakers of different ages used the language to determine whether there was a change in progress (which there was). Labov was interested in a feature of Vineyarder speech in which the diphthongs [ɑi] as in *right* and [ɑu] as in *out* are *centralized*, sounded more like 'roit' and 'oot,' respectively.[1] This centralization was a historical feature of the island dialect but may have been increasingly influenced by the mainland pronunciation as more mainlanders used the island for summer vacations. Labov found an interesting pattern in which overall, the younger speakers were actually using more centralization than the older group, except for the very youngest group.

His demonstration that one could observe change in progress was important, but even more important was his exploration of the **social motivation** behind the change. He wanted to see what kinds of people (in addition to younger islanders) were using this centralization more, and he found that in general, it was used most by the fisherman in one part of the island and by people who had a "positive orientation" to the island. For younger speakers, those who were planning on staying on the island in the future used it more. So he argued that the centralization was used by those who had more of an "islander" identity.

In subsequent work, Labov and other researchers refined their techniques and added gender as one of the social identity categories included in their studies. As Labov (2001) frames it, gender is one of the characteristics that might allow linguists to specify who the leaders of language change are. Labov and others try to find very general patterns in language change, and gender fits into that. In much of the work we've looked at in this book, gender was the primary focus of research, but here it is only important insofar as it explains language change.

A little terminology is important to understand how these studies work. In each study, there is a focus on a **sociolinguistic variable**. A sociolinguistic variable is often defined as "more than one way of saying the same thing." For example, in the Martha's Vineyard study, one of the variables was the pronunciation of the vowel in words such as *right, side, abide, fine, kite*, and so on. So any specific utterance of a word with one of these vowels was said to have a **token** of the **variable** (ɑi) (variables like this are always written inside parentheses). Note that **variables** are not the same as **variants**. The variants are the possibilities for each variable. For (ɑi), the variants were centralized and non-centralized. Another variable commonly studied in English is the *-ing* ending on multisyllabic words such as *talking*. In this example, the variable can be written as (-ing), and the two (most common) variants are [ɪŋ] (*walking*) and [ɪn] (*walkin'*). We find variables in almost every 'level' of language. The examples so far have all been about phonological variables, having to do with sound, but there are also morphological, syntactic, pragmatic, and lexical variables, and all have been found to be sensitive to gender.

'Canonical' gender patterns in the binary

Since Labov's study in 1963, the study of variation has grown significantly, so that at this point in the field's history, some generalizations can be made about what kinds of patterns tend to recur. By 'patterns' I mean quantitative patterns: What groups use what variants more or less? Gender is one of the most prominent social dimensions on which these generalizations have been made.[2] The way gender has been conceived in this subfield has until recently been entirely binary and assuming a biological determinism for gender behavior (indeed, many studies still use the term *sex* for gender), mainly because of a view of society in categorical terms, which is entailed by the variationist method. That is, in order to count things, you need clear categories to put them into, and since gender comes 'already categorized' as men and women, that's how it usually works for gender. As we will see, at least in some corners of this subfield, the methods of analysis have caught up with more contemporary theorizations of gender, such as the performativity and indexicality mentioned in earlier chapters (indeed, the 'Eckert' of Eckert and McConnell-Ginet who introduced the term **Community of Practice** to language and gender is a variationist sociolinguist). However, the general patterns and principles of studies of variation and change are formed in ways that see gender as a strict binary, with women tending to act one way and men the opposite way.

Labov's principles of linguistic change

Early on in the history of variationist sociolinguistics, Labov (1966) focused more on how changes moved through the socioeconomic class structure of a community. He suggested that one kind of change started with the upper classes and was then adopted by lower classes. This kind of change he called a **change from above**. However, in a **change from below**, it is the working class (technically, Labov says it is the second-lowest class) that holds the leaders of the change, and the change eventually moves up to the upper classes. So, in Labov's classification, there are the two types of change, from above and from below. There is also variation that is **stable**. That is, the amount of use for one variant is about the same from generation to generation. The (-ing) variable is an example of a stable variable, as it has been in English for centuries, and although the rates seem to move around, they generally don't go in a particular direction by age. For example, we as linguists can't make a generalization that older people are using [ɪŋ] more than young people.

   Labov (2001) suggests a set of Principles of Language Change, and one set of those principles has to do with gender.

Table 7.1 Principles of language change for gender, traditional formulation

Stable variables	Women use more of the 'standard' variable than men (where the 'standard' variable is usually whatever the upper class uses most)
Changes from above	Women use more of the incoming form than men (where the incoming form is the form used most by the younger generations)
Changes from below	Women use more of the incoming form than men

Adapted from Labov (1990, 2001).

Table 7.2 Principles of language change for gender, alternate formulation

Stable variables	Men use more of the 'stigmatized' variable than women (where the 'stigmatized' variable is usually whatever the lowest class uses most)
Changes from above	Men use more of the outgoing form than women (where the outgoing form is the form used most by the older generations)
Changes from below	Men use more of the outgoing form than women

Adapted from Labov (1990, 2001).

Note that all of these principles are formulated as women doing something differently than men. It's important to notice this because it implies that somehow the men have the unmarked way of behaving. The principles could just as easily be formulated the other way around.

In addition, explanations for the patterns generally tend to be formulated more for women's behavior than men, as we will see below. By writing the principles in the second way, men are presented as the 'problematic' group that needs explanation as much as women.

Nevertheless, let's work through these principles with some examples for better understanding. For the first principle, Labov says that for **stable variables**, women use more of the 'standard' than men. An example of this comes from the variable (-ing). In most studies that have been done (and there have been many), women use more of the [ɪŋ] variant and men use more of the [ɪn] variant. The former is seen as the 'standard' variant because it is also used more often by speakers who are upper class and more educated. The [ɪŋ] variant also matches more closely the written version.

Another example of a stable variable is syllable-final *-s* in Spanish, which has been studied almost as much as (-ing) in English, beginning with Cedergren (1973), who studied this variable in Panama. For this variable, which seems to be present at some level in all varieties of Spanish, /s/ is 'weakened' to [h] or even deleted altogether. Poplack (1980, p. 55) provides the example from Puerto Rican Spanish of *las cosas bonitas* 'the pretty things,' which is also sometimes said *la cosa bonita* even though it seems like it could lead to misunderstanding. In general, working class people delete the /s/ more often, and men delete more than women, but there usually isn't a difference in rates by age. For example, Kapović (2017) finds a very strong pattern in which men show about half as much full /s/ articulation as women. At the same time, more educated people overall use more /s/.

A study of **change from above** can be seen in Brian Brubaker's (2012) study of Taiwanese Mandarin. Taiwan has a distinctive dialect of Mandarin but has increasingly adopted the Beijing pronunciation to be the prestigious one. Beijing Mandarin has a much more **retroflexed** way of pronouncing **sibilants**, which means that sounds like /s/ and /z/ sound more like <sh> in *mesh*, and a /z/ sounds like how the <s> is pronounced in *measure*. Brubaker shows that the retroflexed pronunciation is increasing in Taiwan across generations, especially among more educated Taiwanese. This change is therefore a change from above because the upper classes – as measured by education – are adopting the change faster than lower classes. As shown in Figure 7.1, women are more likely to use the new variant (used by younger people, in this case retroflexed pronunciation) and men are more likely to use the old variant (used more by older people). This is an example of Labov's principle in Table 7.1 that women lead in change from above (women are said to be *leading* because they are adopting the new way of speaking before men).

Finally, **changes from below** are those that first appear in the lower classes and are later adopted by upper classes. An example of this kind of change comes from a study in the 1980s on intonation in Australian English (Guy et al. 1986). In this study, the authors were interested in an intonation pattern in which there is a rising intonation on statements, which they called **Australian Questioning Intonation** (AQI; elsewhere more generically called **High Rising Tone** [HRT]). Once again,

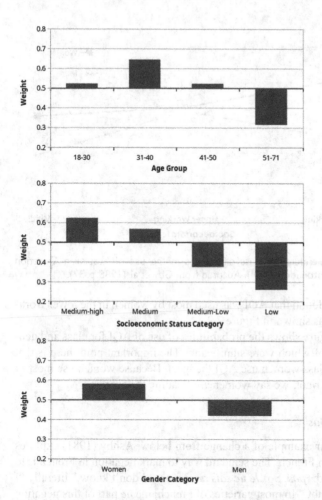

Figure 7.1 Probability weights for the use of retroflexion in Taiwanese Mandarin across three social variables. Adapted from Brubaker (2012, p. 75–86).

the researchers first established that there was a change in progress by noting that the speech of teenagers had more of the intonation pattern than the older speakers in their sample from Sydney, Australia, and by comparing their data with a corpus of speech gathered in the 1960s.

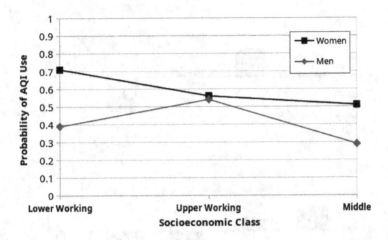

Figure 7.2 Gender and class differences in the use of Australian Question Intonation (AQI). Adapted from Guy et al. (1986, p. 37).

They also found that AQI was used most by women in the lower working class, as shown in Figure 7.2.

This figure shows the probabilities of use of AQI for class and gender, both of which were significant.[3] The important point here is that working-class women use AQI the most. Because women use most of the new variant, we say women are 'leading the change.'

Interactions

In a similar example of a change from below, Ashby (1981) explores negation in French. The standard way to mark negation in French is to use *ne*+verb+*pas*. So, *Je ne sais pas* means "I don't know," literally "I not know not." In most varieties of French, the *ne* part of this negation can be sometimes reduced or deleted, so the sentence becomes *Je sais pas*, "I know not." Ashby finds that *ne*-deletion occurs most among younger and working-class speakers, as well as women. But he also found an **interaction pattern**: there was an insignificant difference between genders among older and upper-class speakers, but the difference between genders was prominent for everyone else. So what was the explanation? We can't compare all men and all women; we have to include the socioeconomic group they are also part of. The interpretation of this pattern is that at the beginning of this change from below, women move away from men, and then eventually men catch up. Penelope Eckert (1989) identifies a pattern of interaction for stable variables as well. In the lowest class, women use more of the variants used by lower-class speakers than men do (which goes against Labov's first principle above), but in the middle and upper classes, men use the more of the same variant that women use. The point is that in many situations, the effect of gender is not the same for all subgroups such as class or race or age.

It's important to remember that none of these generalizations are categorically true everywhere, and there are cases in which the opposite pattern is true for each of these generalizations. In places where status and class structure are different from the studies I just discussed, they prove challenging to use in an analysis (and the vast majority of variation studies have been done in places with very similar status and gender categories). So these patterns of change are not an inevitable feature of language and gender, but are affected by the ways that class, age, and gender are indexed through language in different societies.

One example of a different pattern comes from Jack Sidnell's (1999) study of how speakers in a village in Guyana express the first person singular, choosing among *ai*, *a*, or *mi*. *Ai* would be most equivalent to a 'standard.' But Sidnell found that men tended to use this form more than women, which goes against Labov's first principle. In a different study, Niloofar Haeri (1997) faced a different continuum of standardization because in her analysis of a community in Egypt, in addition to a vernacular Arabic and Modern Standard Arabic, speakers were influenced by Classical Arabic, the language of the Islamic Holy Book, the Quran.

One other important pattern explains an interaction between the gender and class categories and variation. In a few studies, gender has a different pattern for the speakers in the lowest class than for any other class. That is, for a stable variable, women of the lowest class use most of the 'non-standard' variant (the one use more generally by lower-class speakers) and middle- to upper-class men use more of the same 'non-standard' variant than middle- to upper-class women.

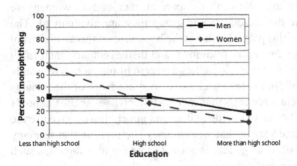

Figure 7.3 Probability of the use of the local variant for the (aw)-monophthongization in Pittsburgh.

For example, in my data from Pittsburgh shown in Figure 7.3, you can see that the women of the lowest socioeconomic class (measured using their occupation) use more '/aw/-monophthongization' than men; **/aw/-monophthongization** is the local Pittsburgh way of saying sounds in words like *down* and *out*, which sounds like 'dahn' and 'aht' when monophthongized. (aw), as I call the variable, is involved in a change from above in Pittsburgh, as middle-class speakers are rapidly moving away from it (see Johnstone and Kiesling 2008 and Johnstone 2013). So most of the pattern, in which women are using less of the old 'non-standard' variant, is an example of the principles above. However, the lowest-class group shows a reverse of this pattern. This pattern is found elsewhere as well, as pointed out by Eckert (1989).

A final caveat about all of these generalizations about patterns of language use is that these are just **correlational** patterns; they do not mean anything until researchers (or anyone else) provides explanations for why the patterns recur. For example, just because upper-class speakers and women do something at a similar rate doesn't necessarily mean that the variant has a meaning like 'prestige' or 'femininity' attached to it; and even though this correlation between gender and class is generally taken to mean that women are using more of a prestigious variant, there's no reason we can't say that upper class speakers are more likely to use a feminine variant. So, that warning given, let's look at some of those explanations.

Explanations for gender patterns in variation

Over the years, researchers have presented a good number of explanations for the patterns mentioned above. Some of them are more general patterns for language change and variation, but most of those have incorporated the gender patterns as well, so I'll explore all of those. I'll first turn to what I would consider 'traditional' or 'canonical' explanations, and then look at some more recent explanations before considering the ways that the more recent explanations have improved on the earliest, relatively all-encompassing ones.

Traditional explanations

Women's advantage in verbal ability

The idea that women are more verbally adept than men, and that this causes them to lead in language change, is an old one and is often mentioned. Probably the most complete argument for this idea comes from Jack Chambers (1995). The idea is that there is some genetic predisposition for women and girls to pay more attention to language and linguistic form than men, who can't appreciate the subtleties of how important and valuable linguistic form is for social reputation. This is a pretty mechanical explanation in the sense that it should apply equally everywhere. Chambers argues that the advantage doesn't have to be large for it to have the effects it does. The problem is that complex behaviors such as 'verbal ability' are tricky to define, and even trickier to tie to any kind of biological trait. There's no 'smoking gun' evidence beyond tests and other correlations of girls/women and boys/men to support the argument, and by then, culture would have had an effect that could overwhelm biology. It also seems that a biological cause would produce a more consistent effect for all kinds of verbal abilities. It's also worth noting that this is an idea that supports hiring more women into positions such as telephone sales and support. Deborah Cameron (2008) describes this connection which she shows is clearly based in ideology and not biology.

More evidence that such a strong biological determinism fails to explain the data, as well as not having a clear mechanism, comes from work by Terttu Nevalainen and Helena Raumolin-Brunberg (2016), who analyze real-time data for a number of changes in English from the 15th through the 18th century. That is, they actually look at how the language is used at different points in time (a **real-time** study), as opposed to looking at differences across generations at one time (an **apparent time** study). This is an important study that analyzes the personal correspondence of around 800 people from this period. Letters of this sort are the closest we can get to evidence of the vernacular speech that most people actually used in a given historical period, as they are sometimes intimate records of people talking directly to one another. In Nevalainen and Raumolin-Brunberg's study, a number of changes are inspected for the ways that changes of this period spread through the letters (see also the summary in Gregoire 2006). The majority of these changes are indeed led by women, but most of those that are led by women do not develop a gender differentiation until the overall use of the new variant reaches about 30 percent. For example, in Figure 7.4, we see the rise of the use of *my* and *thy* as opposed to *mine* and *thine*. Note that the gender rates are virtually identical, with men using a little more of the new variant until 1460 to 1499, when the overall usage passes around 30 percent.

They find a similar pattern for the rise of the use of the possessive *its* rather than *it*, a change that only arises in the 17th century. Nevalainen

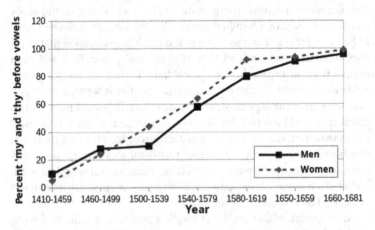

Figure 7.4 The rise of the pronouns my and thy in 40-year increments. Adapted from Nalainen and Raumolin-Brunberg (2016, chapter 6).

and Raumolin-Brunberg show that there is basically no difference in use by gender until after 1659, when the rates climb above 30 percent.

These patterns are important counterarguments to the biological explanation, because we would expect that the 'advantage' of women would be true throughout a change and not only once it reaches as particular level. This is true of studies of apparent time as well. For example, Eckert (2000) analyzes multiple vowel changes and finds that whether gender differences show up are a function of the age of a change, with the newest changes not participating in gender differentiation. So clearly some sort of meaning needs to get attached to the old and new forms – recall from Chapter 4 that we would say that the forms need to become **indexed** to gender or some other social value.

Prestige

One possible value that has been proposed is **prestige**. People want to use language that has prestige, which in this research paradigm generally means the speech used by more upper-class speakers as well as the language used when speakers are paying more attention to their speech. Later we'll explore prestige a little more, but in general, it's the assumption that everyone wants to talk like the most educated and upper-class speakers, and that women want to do that more than men. Of course this doesn't explain women's lead in changes from below (in which the change starts in the lower classes, a contrast that Labov [1990, 2001] calls the **gender paradox**), but in those cases, the idea is that the changes are below the level of awareness and no one has noticed them yet (which means that there needs to be another explanation for women using new ways of speaking before men).

An interesting corollary to this is the idea of **covert prestige**, a term proposed by Labov (1966) but demonstrated by Peter Trudgill (1972). The idea is that language used more by working-class speakers has some kind of prestige attached to it, but it's a prestige that is not overtly admitted by speakers, so it is 'covert.' Nevertheless, it can be discovered by asking speakers how they think they talk and comparing it with how they actually talk. If they over-report using language associated with upper-class speakers, then they orient to prestige, but if they under-report using those, then they are orienting to covert prestige. Trudgill used this exact process and found that men tended to under-report their use of the prestige variant, while women over-reported their use. He argued that there is something of value for men in using 'non-standard' or 'vernacular' variants, while women did not gain that value.

But covert prestige is an odd term – it could simply be called 'solidarity,' as the men are not communicating some special unknown or secret prestige connected to a secret society (which is what the term 'covert' suggests to me), but rather probably using the vernacular to show that they are connecting to the people they are talking to, without trying to appear too uppity. We'll see more evidence for this when we explore some of the studies that have investigated norms through perception experiments.

So prestige and covert prestige do offer some meaningful social arguments about why people use particular linguistic variants, but we might then wonder *why* men are more likely to orient to solidarity and women more toward (socioeconomic) prestige, and also how forms end up getting associated with prestige and gender in the first place, since there is nothing in these studies to suggest that the gender difference didn't come first. We will be able to tease this apart in later sections.

Linguistic insecurity

One way that prestige has been operationalized is through the notion of **linguistic insecurity**. Linguistic insecurity is the concept that people have ideas about 'correct' language use, but don't always think they themselves speak in the 'correct' way.[4] Insecurity describes when people think that their pronunciation does not match the 'correct' pronunciation (much like the over-reporting above). It is suggested that this belief leads to **hypercorrection**, in which people generalize a 'correct' form to a situation that doesn't really call for it, or when people use more of the 'correct' form than the people they are assumed to be emulating. For example, when people say *between you and I* in English, this is a hypercorrection of saying *you and me* in subject position, as in *you and me don't agree much. Between you and me* is actually 'correct' because the pronouns are the object of the preposition *between*. In Labov's (1966) original formulation, the hypercorrection is quantitative, with middle-class speakers using more of the prestige variant than even the highest-class speakers. So, there's an argument that women are more linguistically insecure and that's why they lead sound changes and use more prestigious variants than men. There's not too much discussion of why this linguistic insecurity might exist, but a subtler argument that does have some explanation is provided by Eckert (1989), which I will discuss later.

Social networks and accommodation

Lesley Milroy (1980) brought to these explanations the idea that perhaps people who have more friends, or closer friends, might use variables differently. She investigated how people in Belfast, Northern Ireland, use different vowel changes depending on their **social networks**. These are similar to the online social networks you may familiar with but are measured based on 'real life' connections. People are said to have **dense** networks if the network has lots of people who know each other and who have friends who are also friends with each other. Networks are more **multiplex** if people know each other in different ways, such as working together and also being friends outside of work. Milroy found that more dense and multiplex networks promoted the use of vernacular variants and that networks connected through loose ties (that is, not very densely connected) promoted language changes. In terms of gender, she found that in a neighborhood in which the men had denser networks, the men used more of the vernacular variants. This is a pretty mechanical explanation, because it basically says that if you have a denser and multiplex network, you'll use more vernacular. It doesn't say anything about *why* those people or neighborhoods are more dense and multiplex in the first place. But it does give clues about how changes might spread, so we might find that generally women have more loose ties and men have more dense and multiplex networks. The trick then would be to explain why men and women have different kinds of networks.

Although network studies don't look into the 'black box' of the network to see *why* these ties are working as they do, it has been shown in other studies that people tend to **accommodate** to people they spend time with and are socially attracted to. There's a whole theory around this idea known as **Communication Accommodation Theory**, which focuses on theorizing how and when speakers **converge** and **diverge** in interaction. One intriguing study (Namy et al. 2002) suggested that women are more likely to accommodate than men, and that women are more likely to accommodate to men than women. They had speakers shadow (immediately repeat) words that they heard from a specific speaker. They then asked other participants to judge whether the repeated utterance was closer to the stimulus than an earlier, non-shadowing utterance. Women were judged to have moved significantly more toward the pronunciations they were listening to. The authors suggested that this result means that women in general pay more attention to variation and their indexical meanings than men do. On the other hand, a more recent study (Pardo 2006) measured convergence between two participants in the context of giving directions on a map and found the opposite pattern. All of these experiments tend to suggest that accommodation plays a role in interaction, but that it is highly sensitive to the attention the speaker puts on how the other person is talking and also to what extent the potential accommodater feels some connection to the other speaker. So if there are sociocultural reasons to pay more attention to a way of speaking for one gender than the other, then they will likely converge more than other speakers. In terms of the gender pattern articulated above, the experimental results suggest that the repeated finding of women's lead in language changes has to do with their position in society in which linguistic form is more important for them than for men, that is, it has more serious social consequences.

Child-rearing patterns

Labov (2001) takes the idea of women leading sound change to be more fundamental and tries to explain this lead through patterns of language acquisition and child care. He argues that women provide the majority of child care, and thus he assumes that children initially learn their language largely from women. This fact means that each younger generation will speak more like women and less like men. Therefore, if women speak in any way differently from men, future generations will move in the women's direction. Labov (2001, p. 308) suggests that this difference is further largely created when working-class men "retreat" from or "resist" women's new ways of speaking. However, he doesn't really explain how or why the women would be speaking differently from the men in the first place, or how or why the men would retreat from those changes. The answer to these questions would require a look at how meaning gets infused into the different variants and related to masculinity and femininity, while the overall explanation proposed by Labov is meant to be much more mechanical. (The pattern hasn't been tested in cultures such as the Samoan and Kaluli described in the previous chapter, which would predict that there would be less of a women's lead for gender because of the different child rearing patterns.)

Linguistic marketplace

The linguistic marketplace explanation suggests that using a particular way of speaking indexes a value in some markets, often thought of in terms of an employment market, although it could be another market such as the **heterosexual market** (see Eckert 2000). In this view, language serves as **symbolic capital**, as opposed to capital in terms of material wealth. Someone with more symbolic capital may be able to turn this into actual capital, but it is not necessary for this conversion to happen – for some people the goal is to have things like 'moral authority' and not material wealth. The idea of a linguistic marketplace was introduced into studies of sociolinguistic variation by Sankoff and Laberge (Sankoff and Laberge 1978), who found that people who had jobs that required the use of 'standard' language were more likely to use that kind of language. This can be extended to the observation that women use more prestigious language, which suggests that perhaps women engage in this market more often than men. That is, they argued that men work at jobs that don't require them to present themselves such that they will be evaluated more highly in their jobs if they use 'standard' language, because manual labor jobs are based on doing manual labor, which can be done well or poorly no matter how you talk. Thus, people who have jobs that are more focused on manual labor will be less involved in the linguistic marketplace. Basically, workers who spend more time talking with customers, and especially those whose job it is to speak with customers, will be more involved in the linguistic marketplace and likely use language that is more 'standard.'

Sylvie Dubois and Barbara Horvath (1999) showed that this approach works in situations where there is actually pressure from different linguistic markets for women and men. They investigated the influence of **Cajun French** on English spoken in Louisiana. They found a striking case of gender divergence in language change, in which women in general are moving away from the 'Cajun' (French-influenced) ways of speaking toward more 'standard' Southern American English ways of speaking. Older speakers tended to show little or no gender differentiation, while younger groups showed a divergence. Most importantly, this difference is not simply a case of women moving toward the 'standard,' but of men moving toward the Cajun variants. Figure 7.5 shows this pattern clearly, with the difference in nasalized vowels sharply increasing among young men.

Dubois and Horvath argued that this divergence is related to the difference in how men and women participate in the economy after what they call the "Cajun Renaissance." They explain that in the 1980s, there was a revaluing of practices from historically Cajun

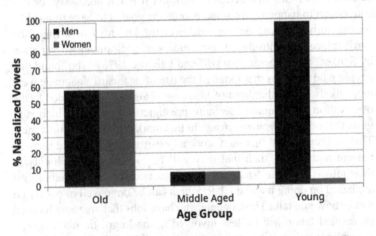

Figure 7.5 Percentage of the Cajun variant of the nasalization variable in Louisiana. Adapted from Dubois and Horvath (1999, p. 294).

communities, beginning with cuisine. Once stigmatized as backward, all of a sudden Cajun culture carried a form of prestige. As this renaissance spread, tourism began to become a larger part of the economy in southern Louisiana. But men and women participated in this economy differently. Men were seen as the stereotypical Cajun, while a female Cajun stereotype is really nowhere to be found. This meant that the roles of men and women in engaging with tourists were different. It paid off for men to act – and talk – as Cajun as possible, working as tour guides and representatives of the Cajun identity that the tourists came to engage with. On the other hand, the women were more likely to act in the customer service realm, staffing gift shops, for example. For the women, then, the more valued way of speaking would be the more corporate 'standard' language and *not* the Cajun way of speaking. The valuable focus of this study is that it is not necessarily the women's participation in the linguistic marketplace that is important, but the men's, and we find an important effect of that participation in the revitalization of a Cajun accent.

So the linguistic marketplace is useful for understanding the way adults use variation, but much of the impetus for changes comes from younger speakers, especially adolescents. What could be the motivation for teenagers to have gender differences in variation norms in, for example, high school? Penelope Eckert (1989, 2000) argues that a different market plays a role (in the US at least) beginning just before the teenage years and puberty: the **heterosexual market**. She notes that in this market, the men compete with men and women with women, so that the value of one way of speaking over another is especially what it says about what kind of man or woman you are in this market. In her analysis of different vowel pronunciations in a high school near Detroit, she found that for some of the changes, the class difference within the girl group was much larger than the class difference within the boy group. Eckert argues that the reason for this pattern is that how the girls present themselves is more important for things like their moral reputation than for the boys. For boys, however, Eckert argues that the market is less about the persona they present in terms of a moral reputation than the things they do, such as sports achievements. Eckert's work has been extremely important for understanding the ways that gender and variation interact, and we will return to it soon.

But for now, note that her argument supports the idea that one reason men and women might use variants differently is that different variants are valuable for one group and not the other, depending on the market and the way that the variables are interpreted.

Intersections, practice, and social meaning

This interpretation is one of the important directions that theoretical advances in the study of variation have taken generally, and especially with regard to gender. The question has been framed in terms of how speakers recognize and create 'social meaning' in linguistic variation. Recall the notions of indexicality, performativity, and communities of practice from Chapter 4. 'Social meaning' is essentially another way of saying 'indexicality,' and an exploration of indexical meaning has been especially important for a better understanding of gender differentials in variation. Also important has been the notion that gender is embedded in other social categories and identities (class, race, ethnicity, etc.), some of them unique to various communities of practice.

Eckert's (2000) study has been central to this development. As mentioned earlier, her study focuses on a high school in suburban Detroit, Michigan. She chose this site because she was interested in the idea that kids, and especially adolescents, are the main drivers of linguistic change.[5] She spent over a year in the high school, not in any classroom but in the spaces outside the classroom, interviewing the students and trying to understand how language fits into their social lives and practices. You might notice that the term **practice** has come back (recall the discussion of **communities of practice** in Chapter 4). Her analysis shows how linguistic variation fits into other practices of Detroit high school students, such as what school activities they engaged in, what they did after school, and even where they hung out during lunchtime. She found that, in addition to gender, the school was organized around two main social categories: *jocks* and *burnouts*. The jocks were more middle class and college oriented, did more school activities, and were more oriented to activities in the school in general than the burnouts. The burnouts were more oriented to resistance, transgression, and the outside adult world, as well as to the urban center of Detroit, than jocks. The other group defined by the students was the *in-betweens*, and actually comprised the largest group of students in the school. Eckert determined these groups by talking to students and charting their networks, showing how the most jock-oriented students clustered together and the most burnout-oriented students also clustered together. But even though the vast majority of students were not in the jock or burnout networks, this difference was the one that all students seemed to orient to as social poles and social evaluation. Eckert even identified one girl's group as the 'burned out burnouts.'

Eckert then showed that ways of speaking at the school correlated with the practices that were typical of the jock and burnout speakers. The other important category at the school was gender, and gender intersected with the jock-burnout distinction in important ways. Eckert argues that gender has more to do with differences of power than anything else, in which "femininity is a culturally-defined form of mitigation or denial of power, whereas masculinity is the affirmation of power" (1989, p. 257). She makes a distinction between status and power, in which status is the construction of symbolic capital in a market, and in the heterosexual marketplace, gender more often involves competing within gender categories than across. From this observation, Eckert makes the prediction that linguistic variation would be greater for girls than boys at the high school, as the boys can construct their power and status through accomplishments, while such accomplishments provide less payoff for girls. "Women ... are constrained to exhibit constantly who they are rather than what they can do, and who they are is defined with respect primarily to other women" (1989, p. 259). So, to put it simply, women will compete more with each other through status than men: "Deprived of power, women can only gain compliance through the indirect use of a man's power or through the development of personal influence. Since to have personal influence without power requires moral authority, women's influence depends primarily on the painstaking creation and elaboration of an image of the whole self as worthy of authority" (1989, p. 256).

The situation that Eckert analyzes linguistically is more complex than in other studies because Eckert studies an entire cluster of variables, most notably the vowels involved in what linguists call the **Northern Cities Chain Shift** (Gordon 2005), in which six vowels are shifting their pronunciation in the cities in the north of the US (such as Detroit,

Chicago, Buffalo, Rochester, and Cleveland, among others). This shift starts with one vowel and then the others change their pronunciation in a chain reaction to the first. So the changes are said to have different 'ages,' with the initial vowel change being the oldest. This is important because Eckert finds that the strength of the gender and jock/burnout differences has to do with the age of the vowel change: newer changes show jock-burnout differences and older changes show gender differences. Eckert then looks at differences in pronunciation in a four-way distinction, but most importantly, she examines the difference between jocks and burnouts within each gender category. She asks: How different were jock girls from burnout girls, and how different were jock boys from burnout boys? Her results are outlined in Figure 7.6.

The variables are arranged with the oldest on the right and the newest on the left. For the oldest variables – that is, (ae) and (a) – the jock/burnout differences are not statistically significant, although they are sensitive to gender overall, a point we'll return to in a minute. The newest change is (e) (the vowel in *bed* and *bet*). The overall differences here are smallest, and most sensitive to the jock/burnout split.

The next change is (uh) (in words like *but* and *bud*). Here the jocks are more different from the burnouts, but importantly, the difference for the girls is much larger than for the boys; (oh) (*off*, *lost*, *talk*) shows

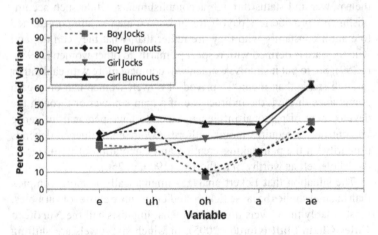

Figure 7.6 Use of advanced variants in Belten High by gender and social group. Adapted from Eckert (1989, p. 262).

even more of an increased difference overall for gender, but while the girls make a big jock/burnout distinction, the boys make hardly any at all. Finally, for (a) (*cot, father*) and (ae) (*bat, bad*), we see that these oldest changes have become differences just in terms of gender; the jock/burnout differences are not significant.

The newest change shows differences between jock and burnouts that are the same in both genders. But the middle-aged changes show what Eckert predicts: The girls show a much greater difference than the boys for differences between jock and burnout. Although they are sensitive to gender difference, the oldest variables are not very sensitive to the category of jock and burnout.

For gender and variation and change, this finding has three very important points. The first is that variables are sensitive to different kinds of social categories at different times, which means we can't make generalizations overall about all stages of change. Second, we can't talk just about gender – we need to talk about gender and class together, at the same time, because they are not independent of each other for all variables. Finally, we need to realize that generalizations are not just about more or less, but sometimes about overall difference. Taking these three points together, we see that the issue of variation and gender has to do with what boys/men and girls/women do with variation within the context of their community. Returning to the idea of communities of practice, we can see that the *norms* and meanings of the variables are not fixed but change as the community uses them to do different social work. Eckert's work has led variationists more generally to look at how variables get indexed with social meaning in the communities they study, which we turn to next.

Meaning in variation

Indexicality, style, and stancetaking

Eckert and her students' work thus suggested that researchers in language variation and change had to think more carefully about how to connect meanings with other social identities, groups, processes, ideologies, and institutions, and more importantly, how speakers themselves infuse meaning into the choice of variants used in interaction. In terms of gender, this view means that just because a variable correlates with gender does not necessarily mean that the variable directly indexes that gender. Recall the notion of indirect indexicality developed by Ochs (1992) (see the section on Performativity and indexing gender in Chapter 4). The idea is that we have ideologies about what kinds of acts, stances, and activities compose gender, and that linguistic items are more likely to index those acts, activities, and stances than directly index masculinity and femininity.

My study of men in a fraternity provides an example of this (Kiesling 1998). I measured the individual rates of (ing) use for each of the ten men in the fraternity in three main interactional contexts: socializing, which comprises things like parties and casual, everyday talk; one on one interviews with me; and talk in their weekly meetings. The general pattern was one in which the men used, on average, the most [ɪn] during socializing, less in interviews, and the least in meetings. The interesting thing about the difference between socializing and meetings is that the men were basically talking to the same people but in different situations, so they must have been thinking that they were *doing* something different in those two situations. Even more interesting is that the individual differences became greater in the meeting than anywhere else. You can see this in Figure 7.7.[6]

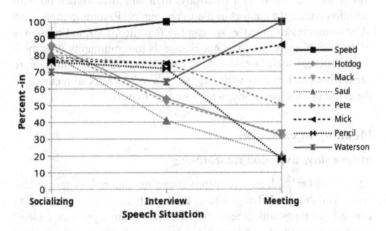

Figure 7.7 Use of (ing) in progressive verb forms by speaker and speech activity. Adapted from Kiesling (1998, p. 84).

In the figure, every line represents a single individual, and each point a speech situation, so you can see how they differ from situation to situation. They all use [m] pretty much all the time in socializing and then they start to shift in interviews with me and in meetings. Why did the men have such a disagreement about how to use (ing) in these situations when they agreed in the socializing situations? I argued that the difference is because they were generally taking different kinds of stances in these situations, but all were stances that were associated with masculinity in some way. In the meeting, the men who used the least [m] (Ram, Saul, Pencil, Mack, and Art) all created authority through the official structure of the fraternity, for instance, claiming authority to speak and give opinions based on their seniority or the offices they've held. On the other hand, the high [m] users (Pete, Waterson, Mick, and Speed) used that high rate with different kinds of stances and personalities from the other men in varied ways: a hard-working stance, a stance creating solidarity with the people in the meeting, and a stance of resistance or even rebellion against the traditional hierarchies of the fraternity.

So these differing rates can be explained by the way that variants are used to do things like take stances in interaction. But the (ing) rates also show a correlation with gender: The stances that the high [m] users were showing in the fraternity meetings are aligned with a particular kind of masculinity. Moreover, one can imagine that the kind of solidarity-focused, hard-worker identity that the men are creating might generalize to other masculinities, but less so to femininity. We can thus see that the particular gender patterning of variation is connected to stance in this way.

The men also used a collection of other linguistic and non-linguistic strategies to create these stances, a collection of features that Eckert and students (California Style Collective et al. 1993, p. 5) call a personal or group **style**, which they describe as follows:

> The construction of style is a process of **bricolage**. Resources from a broad social landscape will be identifiable not only by which resources it uses, but how it uses each resource and how it combines all its resources. Key to the issue of social reproduction is the fact that the choice of stylistic resources is neither neutral nor random. ... [W]hat these resources have in common is that

they have some kind of meaning for the speaker who takes them up – the bricoleur. The meaning of an element of style for a brico-leur is the product of his or her interpretation of the social signifi-cance of the style that serves as its source.

In the high school study, Eckert takes this observation further to argue that the vowel variables can be mixed and matched to make particular styles, and that individual speakers have agency in how they do that. However, how do those social meanings get into the community of practice? Eckert argues that much of this work takes place through the development of certain **sociolinguistic icons.** For example, in the school, the icons are kids who mark the boundaries of social meaning such as the 'burned out burnout' network, who had the most extreme pronunciations of the vowels, especially the girls of this group. This view argues that when other speakers move toward these extreme variants (even if they don't get all the way to the extreme), they are attaching to themselves part of the style that these recognizable icons are known to have. From this perspective, we can see how patterns of gender are built in a community from the more particular associations with specific people or styles, and these styles conform to (or chal-lenge) different gender stereotypes and ideologies.

Another change where we see a gender difference based on style and stance, and sociolinguistic icons, is the rise of the use of *dude* in the US from the 1970s to the 2000s. This address term was the subject of a paper of mine published in 2004 (Kiesling 2004). This study finds that young men are most likely to use the term, although it has spread to much of the English-speaking population of North America. My argu-ment, based on multiple sources, is that *dude* helps to create a stance of **cool solidarity** which in turn is related to its origins as a term in the 'cool' and male-dominated subcultures of surfing and skateboarding. These cultures produced a kind of laid-back, cool, unconcerned, socio-linguistic icon for the term, which anyone who used the term would incorporate to give them that cool and friendly style. So, in *dude*, we see stance, style, and sociolinguistic icon coming together to 'do' cool solidarity in interaction.

All of these studies and theorizing suggest that in order to under-stand the norms of language use and why language norms differ by gender, we need to understand whether and how speakers orient to these meanings. There are a few experimental studies that show that these meanings are complex and powerful, but also that they change depending on who we think is talking. Moreover, one of the most important categories of speaker for the studies that have been done has to do with the gender identity of the speaker.

Perceiving gender in speech

You might think that linguistic perception is pretty straightforward; we hear what is in the sound sequence, or see what is in the signed sequence, and so on. However, how we perceive what others produce is affected strongly by who we think is talking. Perceptual effects are shown strongly by the so-called McGurk effect (McGurk and Macdonald 1976), in which someone who is played the sound "ga-ga" but who watches someone saying "ba-ba" hears "da-da." It turns out that when it comes to how people perceive phonological information, what we think of a person is important. A similar effect was obtained by Nancy Niedzielski (1999) using social categories. She was interested to see how Detroiters heard a sound that was used in Detroit. However, Detroiters generally believe that it is used in Canada and not so much in Detroit. The sound is /aw/ as in *about*. Niedzielski played a recording of a speaker to some Detroiters and then asked them to match a recording of a version of that sound to what they just heard. The test was that half the respondents were told that the initial speaker was from Detroit and half were told that they were from a Canadian city just across the border. The results were striking: The speakers who thought they were listening to a Detroiter were about three times less likely to say (correctly!) that the vowel they heard was the one that is stereotypical of Canadians. This is a very strong effect of starting with a stereotype of the speaker.

The strength of gender perception has been shown similarly. Elizabeth Strand and Keith Johnson (1996) first played a series of words to listeners that differed in pronunciation on a continuum from [ʃɑd] (*shod*) to [sad] (*sod*) and asked which word they heard. They were more likely to say the border between the two was closer to [ʃɑd] when they heard a masculine voice and the opposite when they heard a feminine voice. Moreover, if the voice was heard to be "stereotypically masculine," the border was even further to the [ʃɑd] end (for various reasons, men tend to pronounce the sound more in the direction of the effect). They did another experiment in which they showed a masculine or feminine face before the participants heard the continuum and the pictures had a similar effect to the stereotypical voices. Similar experiments supported these results in Johnson et al. (1999) and Strand (2000).

So it's pretty clear that listeners shift their expectations of how they hear language based on the identity of the person they are talking to. In Niedzielski's case, it was Canadian or American, but in other cases, it had to do with gender. In short, you hear different things depending on whether you think the speaker is a man or woman. Much of this work suggests that the biases in hearing usually have to do with **normalization**: Post-puberty, women tend to have shorter vocal tracts than men of the same size. But if we normalize for this fact – that is, factor this difference out – there's no reason we don't always change our perception somewhat based on what we know about the identity of the people we are talking to. So the same vowel pronunciation might be heard more readily as an 'advanced change' or 'non-standard' if we know we are talking to a woman and expect her to have those features.

That's one way that perception has been studied with respect to gender – basic speech perception is changed by what we know about a speaker's gender. Another way is about how people understand the indexicality of variants and how they assemble judgements about speakers based on how they sound. To understand how people understand the indexical meaning of forms, we can to some extent just ask people. For example, I could ask someone: "If I say 'I'm talkin' to you,' how does your impression of me differ if I say 'I'm talking to you.'" But asking questions like this only goes so far, because people have ideas, for example, about what they are supposed to say, what the experimenter wants them to say, and so on. In other words, their responses aren't very reliable. And the kinds of indexical meaning we have been talking about are pretty subtle.

So this kind of indexicality has been studied in ways that are indirect. In 1960, Wallace Lambert and colleagues published a study (Lambert et al. 1960) that tested the attitudes of Canadians toward

French and English speakers by having the same person record the same passage in French and English, playing one of those versions to a listener, and then asking the listener to rate the speaker on an array of personality traits, where the only difference was the language of the recording (although a number of speakers were used so that listeners did not realize that some of the recordings were by the same speaker). Each of the language recordings is called a 'guise,' and the method is called a **matched guise** study.

Matched guise studies have become more and more sophisticated over time. The most sophisticated to date are those performed by Campbell-Kibler (Campbell-Kibler 2007, 2008, 2009). Her studies of (ing) show a similar malleability of indexical meaning as discussed previously, but also a high degree of contextual dependence. Campbell-Kibler made recordings of eight speakers from California and the US South (North Carolina). She selected a portion of each recording for the experiment and spliced in the sound so that there was a recording that was exactly the same except for (ing), which sounded like *walkin'* in one and *walking* in the other. She then played these recordings and elicited free-form judgements about the speakers, so that she could see what kinds of reactions people had (this is better than just making up a bunch of adjectives about the speaker you think might be used by the listener). She then used recurring adjectives from these reactions, including perceptions of the speaker's region, socioeconomic class, and gender, in the matched guise experiment. While she finds overall patterns, such as [ɪn] guise speakers being seen as more working class, it is the interactions that are most interesting. Here we see, for example, that if speakers are heard as more working class, then listeners judge them to be less intelligent when they are using the [ɪn] variant. However, if a speaker is heard as middle class, then there isn't a difference in the intelligence rating for the different pronunciations of (ing). So how people respond to (ing) in terms of traits like intelligence and stances like 'condescending' depends on who listeners think they are hearing.

Gender made a difference as well. For example, listeners heard one of the speakers in Campbell-Kibler's study, Valerie, as less intelligent when she used the [ɪŋ] pronunciation if they thought she was 'annoying.' If they didn't think she was annoying, they rated her more highly for the [ɪŋ] guise. The differing 'annoying' responses seem to be related to how different listeners orient to the content of her talk – thinking, for example, that complaining about the coursework for her major means that she's not very intelligent. Campbell-Kibler (2008, pp. 644–645) points out that the scope of her study does not make it possible to draw broad conclusions or generalizations about exactly how gender has an effect on meaning, or the indexicality of (ing), in the larger population beyond (mostly White) young adults who go to elite schools in the US (the respondents to her study). But her experiments do show that the idea that a linguistic variant has a single overall indexical meaning is problematic at best. This fact means that we have to look to more particular and diverse causes for any patterns that we find for men and women generally, and that gender patterns are artifacts of local uses of language like the ones I found in my study of the fraternity.

At this point, you may be feeling frustrated that the generalizations that seemed clear at the outset of this chapter have completed their descent into chaos and you've thrown the book across the room. In response to such impending conceptual chaos, Eckert (2008) proposed the notion of the **indexical field**. An indexical field is a representation of *potential* indexical meanings for a linguistic form. Eckert elaborates: "An indexical field is a constellation of meanings that are ideologically linked. As such, it is inseparable from the ideological field and can be seen as an embodiment of ideology in linguistic form. I emphasize here that this field is not a static structure, but at every moment a representation of a continuous process of reinterpretation" (2008, p. 464). In the case of (ing), Eckert proposes that the field is made up of a number ideologically linked oppositions (where the first in every pair is associated with [ɪŋ]), as in Table 7.3.

Table 7.3 Indexical field for (-ing)

[ɪŋ] (working)	[ɪn] (workin')
Educated	Uneducated
Formal	Casual
Effortful	Easygoing/lazy
Articulate/pretentious	Inarticulate/unpretentious

Adapted from Eckert (2008)

I would add intelligent–unintelligent to the educated pair as well. The point is that in any situation, the actual way that a variant is heard depends on all sorts of contextual factors, not the least of which is what is going on in the conversation around it and the gender of the speakers. For example, factors like the topic of the conversation, the speech situation (there is a sense of 'appropriateness' in ways of speaking to the situation), and even things like whether you feel that you were just interrupted may impact how you interpret an utterance and the variable's role in creating that interpretation. Most importantly for the focus of this book, it means that ideologies about speakers may affect an interpretation as well. If you expect men to be easygoing and relaxed, then you are likely to admire an [ɪn]-using man. If we bring Och's (1992) notion of indirect indexicality into the mix, one can see how gender differences in the use of (ing) might accrue based on the field above (which, as Eckert points out, might be different in different places and shift over time).

One question that comes about from the view of the indexical field and indirect indexicality is how the stances and the ways of speaking get connected to different kinds of identity. To some extent, this could happen just because you talk to lots of different people and as a human you have a language-oriented brain that acts as a pretty good statistical processor. But there are also ways that different kinds of identities or **personas** get connected more explicitly, which we take up in the next section.

Creating speaking stereotypes in mass media: Enregisterment

Way back in Chapter 2, we noted that 'regular' people have ideas about language – that people talk about language and the people who use it. So it stands to reason that indexical meanings are not always as implicit as in the situations described previously. In fact, we do explicitly talk about "Droppin' your Gs" and what kind of people do that from time to time. If these ideas are repeated enough, we end up with stereotypes about ways of speaking and specific types of people who speak that way, a process called **enregisterment** by linguists.

A good example of enregisterment is explained by Johnstone (2013), who shows how the local dialect of Pittsburgh, Pennsylvania, became familiar to the local residents, such that it can be used to claim Pittsburgh identity on t-shirts and bumper stickers, among other things.

Before the 1960s, if you went to Pittsburgh, you could definitely hear a unique dialect. But no one in Pittsburgh really knew that or talked about it. It wasn't until how Pittsburghers talked started being noticed outside of Pittsburgh that a thing called *Pittsburghese* really developed, and it really took off once someone wrote a 'dictionary' of Pittsburghese. The popular idea of the Pittsburgh dialect wasn't a natural development, but a cultural one that happened to focus on language. However, it didn't only focus on language, because when the dialect became enregistered, it relied on particular stereotypes of White, working-class Pittsburghers (you can see these in some YouTube videos).[7] The point is that enregisterment is about people overtly connecting a way of speaking to a particular kind of person.

These kinds of enregisterments can happen with gender as well, and these end up being similar to the sociolinguistic icons that Eckert talks about. For example, in the 1980s in the US there emerged a style known as "Valley Girl Talk" which was stereotypically characterized by California vowels, rising intonation in indicative sentences, and frequent use of the discourse marker *like*. This style was extremely well known and imitated, and eventually many of the variants became more widespread, and they were led mostly by girls and women (especially the rising intonation and *like* as a verb to introduce a quotation in a story). Another example is the *Kogal*, a style of young Japanese femininity that arose in the 1990s. Miller (2004) explains that not only does their style challenge traditional Japanese femininity, but the way they talk is in fact one of the things most commented on about their style. And just so you don't think it's always girls with whom this happens, one can certainly see the enregisterment of California 'surfer dudes' as part of the rise of *dude*, and in particular films such as *Bill and Ted's Excellent Adventure* (see Kiesling 2004). These examples show how gender becomes enregistered in very particular ways such that people end up conceptualizing gender through these kinds of enregistered stereotypes. Of course, gender isn't the only identity category that gets enregistered. Sexuality or sexual identity has also been enregistered and I turn to this topic in the next section.

Speaking your sexuality

At the very beginning of the book, I referred to the fact that it is often possible to know if a man is gay (this is often called 'gaydar,' a portmanteau of *gay* and *radar*), especially with respect to speech. That is, there is an enregistered variety in (American) English such that if a man uses a particular way of speaking, he is heard as gay. This is an enregistered variety because there is at least one stereotype that goes along with this 'gay voice': a flamboyant and often effeminate man (among other traits). This portrayal does not encompass homosexual women – lesbians – who don't seem to use the same recognizable register; I'll discuss this asymmetry below. But first let's explore the research that's been done on this 'gay voice' at it is sometimes called and what it might tell us about language and gender.

This register has been noticed for at least a few decades (for an excellent review of the history of how 'gay styles' have been conceived of and studied, see Cameron and Kulick [2003]). In an early stage of research into this phenomenon, there was a kind of search to describe the 'gay voice,' largely through the basic methods of variationist sociolinguistics, as explained above. In other words, researchers recorded gay and straight men and tried to see how the gay men speak differently from the straight men. The problem is that not all gay men sound gay, and some straight men sound gay, so this tended to not work very well. The assumption was that gay men adopted this way of speaking *because* they were gay. The idea was that there was a kind of parallel between the concept of a speech community (such as Pittsburgh or New York) and the 'gay speech community.' The problem is the variability in the way that gay men speak prevents a generalization about the way that gay men speak. This is true even though many of the early studies focused on White, upper-middle-class men, and when one considers the actual diversity of the 'gay community,' such generalizations quickly fall apart.

The more consistent finding is that the 'gay voice' is a register that is, in fact, available to anyone, but that indexes a *particular kind* of gay persona. Some gay men may adopt many of these features much of the time, but most will deploy them strategically. The most interesting result of experiments about this 'gay voice' is the number of different features that have been suspected to index it. The most common linguistic features this work has tested are the pitch level of men's voices (or $F0$), how /s/ is pronounced, the (ing) variable, and various measures of vowels and vowel space. In general, this research has been done by playing voices (words, sentences, or longer sequences) to respondents and asking them to say whether someone sounds gay or straight, although the matched guise procedure has also been used. In most cases, researchers are looking at these features because they are ones that can index gender, and the idea is that the 'gay voice' uses feminine features to index the gay persona. Women have higher pitched voices than men, on average, pronounce /s/ with a more 'front' articulation (as pointed out above for the experiments done by Strand and Johnson), have a lower rate of [ɪn] than men, and have a more dispersed vowel space than men.[8]

As far as pitch, respondents sometimes say that a higher pitch is important, but pitch often doesn't play a role at all (Gaudio 1994, Linville 1998, Smyth et al. 2003, Munson 2007); /s/ is a little more reliable as a cue, but it depends on how it is measured. In general, someone is perceived as more masculine or feminine depending on /s/ pronunciation: a voice that uses a more 'fronted' /s/ is heard as feminine (a fronted /s/ is one that sounds more like *said* and less like *shed* – if you make these two sounds one after the other and don't move your jaw, you can feel your tongue moving forward for *said*). But again, the results of this research are inconsistent. Vowel space as a cue for a gay male identity seems like it might be somewhat reliable, but it has not been extensively measured and is confounded by the fact that it is often involved in ongoing vowel changes, especially the fronting of back vowels in the US (where most of this work has been done); (ing) is probably the least reliable, partially because it has so many possible meanings, as pointed out by Eckert and Campbell-Kibler. But as noted previously, Campbell-Kibler (2011) found that ratings on one dimension, such as masculinity or competence, depended on the ratings of another dimension for the same linguistic feature (for example, a woman who is heard as annoying will be also heard as pretentious in the [ɪŋ] guise). Once again, we see that the indexicality of linguistic features is highly context-dependent. This result is no doubt due to the fact that even when experimenters try to remove context from speech in order to make sense of it, the people responding in the experiment have to create some context for the kinds of indexical meaning the experiments are asking for and not every person imagines the same contexts. So the same linguistic feature may not be noticed in one context, while in another, it may trigger indexicalities associated with a particular kind of gay persona.

We would think that if there is a gay style or 'gay voice,' that there would be more consistency in these findings. So why isn't this the case? In general, the research suggests that the cause of inconsistency lies in the combination of the context dependency of interpretation of single linguistic features such as /s/-fronting and the fact that the gay persona is a stereotype. Therefore, aspects of the 'gay voice' is used as a resource for accomplishing specific types of gay personas. In other words, much of this research has assumed that gay speakers and all listeners have some consistent idea of what this 'gay voice' is. (And they don't.)

Rob Podesva's studies of an individual gay man who he calls Regan (Podesva 2007, 2011) and how he shifts in different situations are particularly important for demonstrating this strategic deployment of linguistic forms to create different kinds of gay personas. In his study, he recorded one gay man in different communities of practice. This work is reminiscent of the fraternity study of (ing) (Kiesling 1998) in that a single person is followed in different situations. However, in this case, Podesva follows one person and carefully measures more than one variable. These include the use of falsetto voice and some aspects of the California Vowel Shift (CVS). The three situations are in social situations that Regan calls "Boys' night out," dinner with a friend, and a meeting with his supervisor at work. Podesva shows that Regan creates a 'gay partier' persona at the boys' night out, and uses the most advanced forms of the CVS and the most falsetto voice, and uses the least of these in the meeting with his supervisor. In other words, he's not always using his 'gay voice' because he's not always being a 'gay partier,' particularly with his boss. That doesn't mean there isn't a 'gay voice' register that Regan can draw on to create the 'gay partier' style, but that the style is used only in some situations.

You can see that this 'gay voice' is enregistered because comics use various linguistic forms to create stereotypical gay characters. The humor around these characters would not work if the voice was not recognized. Shane Lanning (2015) actually measured three possible features of a gay register when comedians performed a gay character – pitch, (s), and (ing). He found inconsistent patterns for all of the features, which were all used by at least one comedian differently when shifting to the gay character. However, there was no single character performed, and Lanning finds reasons for opposite shifts as well.

For example, one comedian lowers their voice rather than raising it, but Lanning explains that this is in the context of producing a 'sexy voice' so that the lowering of pitch makes sense. These results point once again to the problematics of claiming that a single linguistic feature directly indexes sexuality. Rather, some forms sometimes index sexuality if used in the right way (by now, that should be a totally banal conclusion).

Similarly, one of the interesting results that Podesva comments on is the fact that Regan uses aspects of the CVS to create a gay partier style. Simlarly, Eckert (2011) shows that pre-adolescent girls use the same shift to construct a heterosexual identity, albeit one that is used to create exclusivity among the young girls whose interactions she analyzes. Eckert, Podesva, and Lanning's studies all point us to the idea that the different features of language associated with sexuality are involved in indexical fields (discussed above) that might overlap in unexpected ways, especially if they are part of registers that are indexed when they are combined with other aspects of interaction.

So there's no gay voice, but there is a gay voice. That is, there is no one linguistic feature (or even consistent set of features) that index that a man is gay. On the other hand, there are a few linguistic features that can be used to index being gay, because there is a stereotypical gay voice (or possibly voices) that some speakers use when it suits them.

So that's what we know about the 'gay voice' register. But what about lesbians? In other words, why is there an enregistered gay male style that is frequently used even by straight men, while there is no corresponding 'lesbian style'? Cameron (2011) suggests that one reason is that historically lesbians did not form the kinds of communities that gay men did, so that norms of use could not develop. In other words, there were no networks and no communities of practice in which such a style could congeal. On the other hand, if one way of signaling homosexuality is to be more like stereotypes of the 'opposite' gender, then being more masculine for lesbians may just not be as noticeable (nor, perhaps, as dramatic) as being a more effeminate man for gay men. Partly this could be because lesbians are moving toward the more powerful half of the gender binary (that is, they are indexing masculinity). In short, many cultures don't penalize 'tomboys' to the same degree that they do 'sissies.' The short version of this explanation is that the asymmetry of styles is rooted in the gender-power asymmetry and how homosexuality plays into that.

In any case, the study of (or search for) the 'gay style' offers a number of lessons about how we attach gender to linguistic forms, and how the norms of language and gender arise. If there is no 'gay voice,' and no lesbian voice, then what happens to the idea that men overall have different ways of speaking than women? First of all, it suggests that gender may not be the only and definitely not the primary indexical meaning even for variables that show a strong connection to gender. But more importantly, it points to the problematic nature of generalizations about women and men's speech, given that a group composed of roughly half of any population will have even more variability than we just saw for gay men.

So, how then do we end up with the statistical patterns that are shown by women and men, and how can we reconcile the idea that indexicality is highly context dependent and particular? I can imagine you getting ready to give up and say linguists just play semantic games and can't give an answer to a simple question. The problem is that the simple question has a lot of assumptions incorporated in it. The answers come about only if we admit that there is indeterminacy of meaning in language when abstracted away from actual utterances, especially in terms of indexical meanings. But realize also that just because people experience gender and sexual identity categories as very particular in interaction, it does not mean that over time these particular identities don't share some very general traits. The trick is to not think about the identity of, for example, gay men as determining how they will speak. Rather, it's more enlightening to ask, how are the speakers using the potential meanings of various linguistic features in interaction to make all sorts of social meanings that may be related to an enregistered gay identity, including using resources in new ways?

This turns linguistic questions around, even those about language change. The focus changes to how innovative ways of speaking are being used by speakers to accomplish social goals in coordination with other practices, and then how these goals might be different for different kinds of people, some of whom are more masculine and some more feminine. We'll consider this gender diversity some more in the next section, in which we explore several dimensions of gender and sexuality, and the ways that language helps indicate and construct them.

Trans variation

The field of gender studies, and feminists in general, have long strug-
gled to reconcile those who align their social practices and bodies in
ways that don't fit into the dominant categories of gender and sexuality
in society, as well as those who have been 'assigned' a gender category
that feels wrong for them.[9] From early on, Trans people have challenged
the biological basis of gender categories, and the few people working on
the language surrounding Trans people are challenging a lot about the
earliest assumptions that sociolinguists made about gender.

Lal Zimman is at the forefront of these studies. His dissertation traced
the voices of 15 transmasculine people as they transitioned over a year.
Zimman defines *transmasculine* as "an umbrella label that includes
transgender men (i.e. those assigned to a female gender role at birth
who self-identify as men) as well as other individuals who were female-
assigned but who do not identify as women, including some non-binary
individuals (i.e. those who do not identify as strictly female or male)"
(Zimman 2017, p. 341). In another article (Zimman 2014), he writes
about changes in pitch and pronunciation of /s/ over a year of transition,
as they are taking hormones to align it to their more desired masculine
conception of themselves. The most important point Zimman makes is
the diversity of masculinities that are the outcome of the process and
that the transmasculine speakers did not have a homogeneous desired
outcome or goal. This diversity is reflected in both the trajectories of
voice changes over the year and the overall outcome. In both pitch and
/s/-production, the transmasculine speakers range over values that have
been measured across the traditional categories of men and women. The
participants have different labels for what kind of transmasculine person
they are, from simply *man* or *trans man* to *trans boy* and *genderqueer*.
For the purposes of this chapter, one important facet of these self-cate-
gorizations and descriptions is that they also match with diversities of
voice in terms of pitch and /s/ production, although what's even more
interesting is that there isn't necessarily a linear connection between,
for example, how traditionally masculine a speaker is and whether their
linguistic features are more or less masculine.

Rather, Zimman describes a constellation of fluid categorization
dimensions: identity, presentation, assignment, and sexuality. **Gender
identities** are the categories of identity that people identify with, such

as *man* or *male* as well as *transmasculine, trans man, trans boy, genderqueer*, and so on. **Gender presentation** is the semiotic manifestation and "the various ways that an identity like 'man' can be enacted" (2014, p. 200), including how one talks. **Gender assignment** is the category assigned at birth. Zimman shows that each of these dimensions of what we can call gender or masculinity affects the way that /s/ is deployed to create a gender presentation, but that these are not separable from the bodily experiences of transmasculine people. Once again, no one changes their bodies and voices as easily as we change from jeans to formal wear (but they *can* be changed). In a later article, Zimman (2017) shows that one bilingual transmasculine speaker uses very different /s/ articulations in Spanish and English. In fact, they are almost categorically different. This patterning points out the fact that even within a single speaker, the use of a linguistic item such as /s/ can change dramatically if the speaking context changes dramatically enough.

Trans studies like Zimman's tell us about ourselves even (or especially) if we aren't Trans: Speakers do not say things the same way all the time, and we are all always juggling what category the world is putting us in (assignment), adjusting the stance and persona we create in interaction (presentation), and imagining the category we want to be in (identity), not to mention the desires of attraction encompassed in our sexuality. The transmasculine people studied by Zimman are only different from the men I studied in the fraternity in that their range of diversity is wider than in the fraternity, where I still saw multiple ways of being masculine, as shown by the diversity of rates of (ing) in the meeting situation. Together, all of these studies show us that language and gender are not directly and simply related. The patterns we find that appear to be able to be generalized by gender and sexuality hide a vast array of genders and sexualities, expressed for multiple reasons and constrained as well as enabled by complex life courses and socializations. In the last chapter, we'll consider some implications of this diversity and indeterminacy, both for theorizing about language, gender, and sexuality and for how the subject is presented in the media.

Notes

1 These are vowel sounds which shift their pronunciation over the entire vowel; for example, in [ɑi] as *right* the vowel begins with [ɑ] and ends in [i].

2 The patterns described here are based on discussions by Labov, Eckert, and my own textbook on variation (Eckert 1990; Labov 1990; Labov 2001; Kiesling 2011).

3 A **loglinear multiple regression** was used for these data, in which many competing factors predicting AQI use were input into a model, which then selected which factors are the most significant for prediction. This is standard practice in variationist sociolinguistics.

4 I use scare quotes for 'correct' to highlight the fact that 'correct' is an ideological construct and arbitrarily determined.

5 In fact, numerous studies show that kids in European and European-colonized countries speak mostly like their parents until somewhere between about eight and ten years old, when they begin to talk more like their peers than their parents (see, for example, Kerswill 1996).

6 I'm presenting the rates of [ɪn] use for the progressive verb form only because (ing) is very sensitive to grammatical category. The multiple logistic regression I used verifies the statistical significance of the patterns in this figure; see Kiesling (1998) for details.

7 www.youtube.com/user/greganddonny and www.youtube.com/user/pitts-burghdad. There is even an episode of *Greg and Donny* that is basically about enregisterment – *Greg and Donny Have an Accent*.

8 Phoneticians can measure vowels (see Johnson 2012), and then plot them using two of those measurements, known as **F1** and **F2**. F1 basically corresponds to how open the mouth is when the vowel is made (the height dimension), while F2 corresponds with where the peak of the tongue is in the mouth when the vowel is articulated (the front-back dimension).

9 A quick reminder here that that I'm using Trans in the asterisked sense – Trans* – but without the asterisk notation, for reasons discussed in Chapter 3. That is, **Trans** is a cover term not only for people who are not the same gender as assigned at birth, but also others who are not binary trans people but nevertheless challenge the binary and essentialist gender categorization.

References

Ashby, W. J. (1981). The Loss of the Negative Particle *ne* in French: A Syntactic Change in Progress. *Language*, 57(3):674–687.

Brubaker, B. L. (2012). *The Normative Standard of Mandarin in Taiwan: An Analysis of Variation in Metapragmatic Discourse*. PhD dissertation, University of Pittsburgh, Pittsburgh, PA.

California Style Collective, T., Arnold, J., Blake, R., Eckert, P., Iwai, M., Mendoza-Denton, N., Morgan, C., Polanyi, L., Solomon, J., and Veatch, T. (1993). Variation and Personal/Group Style. New Ways of Analyzing Variation Conference 22, Ottawa, Ontario.

Cameron, D. (2008). *The Myth of Mars and Venus: Do Men and Women Really Speak Different Languages?* Oxford University Press, Oxford.

Cameron, D. (2011). Sociophonetics and Sexuality: Discussion. *American Speech*, 86(1):98–103.

Cameron, D. and Kulick, D. (2003). *Language and Sexuality*. Cambridge University Press, Cambridge.

Campbell, L. (2013). *Historical Linguistics: An Introduction*, 3rd edition. Edinburgh University Press, Edinburgh.

Campbell-Kibler, K. (2007). Accent, (ing), and the Social Logic of Listener Perceptions. *American Speech*, 82(1):32–64.

Campbell-Kibler, K. (2008). I'll be the Judge of That: Diversity in Social Perceptions of (ING). *Language in Soci*ety, 37(5):637–659.

Campbell-Kibler, K. (2009). The Nature of Sociolinguistic Perception. *Language Variation and Change*, 21(1):135–156.

Campbell-Kibler, K. (2011). Intersecting Variables and Perceived Sexual Orientation in Men. *American Speech*, 86(1):52–68.

Cedergren, H. J. (1973). *The Interplay of Social and Linguistic Factors in Panama*. Cornell University, Ithaca, NY.

Chambers, J. (1995). *Sociolinguistic Theory: Linguistic Variation and its Social Significance*. Blackwell, Cambridge, MA.

Dubois, S. and Horvath, B. (1999). When the Music Changes, You Change Too: Gender and Language Change in Cajun English. *Language Variation and Change*, 11(3):287–313.

Eckert, P. (1989). The Whole Woman: Sex and Gender Differences in Variation. *Language Variation and Change*, 1:245–267.

Eckert, P. (2000). *Linguistic Variation as Social Practice: The Linguistic Construction of Identity in Belten High*. Blackwell Publishers, Malden, MA.

Eckert, P. (2008). Variation and the Indexical Field. *Journal of Sociolinguistics*, 12(4):453–476.

Eckert, P. (2011). Language and Power in the Preadolescent Heterosexual Market. *American Speech*, 86(1):85–97.

Gaudio, R. P. (1994). Sounding Gay: Pitch Properties in the Speech of Gay and Straight Men. *American Speech*, 69(1):30–57.

Gordon, M. (2005). *Vowel Shifting. Do You Speak American?* www.pbs.org/speak/ahead/change/changin/. Accessed May 22, 2018.

Grégoire, S. (2006). Gender and Language Change: The Case of Early Modern Women.   homes.chass.utoronto.ca/~cpercy/courses/6362-gregoire.htm. Accessed May 18, 2018.

Guy, G., Horvath, B., Vonwiller, J., Daisley, E., and Rogers, I. (1986). An Intonational Change in Progress in Australian English. *Language in Society*, 15(1):23–51.

Haeri, N. (1997). The Reproduction of Symbolic Capital: Language, State, and Class in Egypt. *Current Anthropology*, 38(5):795–816.

Johnson, K. (2012). *Acoustic and Auditory Phonetics*, 3rd edition. Wiley-Blackwell, Malden, MA.

Johnson, K., Strand, E. A., and D'Imperio, M. (1999). Auditory-Visual Integration of Talker Gender in Vowel Perception. *Journal of Phonetics*, 27:359–384.

Johnstone, B. (2013). *Speaking Pittsburghese: The Story of a Dialect*. Oxford University Press, New York, NY; Oxford.

Johnstone, B. and Kiesling, S. F. (2008). Indexicality and Experience: Exploring the Meanings of /aw/-monophthongization in Pittsburgh. *Journal of Sociolinguistics*, 12(1):5–33.

Kapović, M. (2017). Variable Within Variable – Simultaneous Stability and Change: The Case of Syllable-Final s in Cuidad Real. *Borealis*, 6(2):249–283.

Kerswill, P. (1996). Children, Adolescents, and Language Change. *Language Variation and Change*, 8(2):177–202.

Kiesling, S. F. (1998). Men's Identities and Sociolinguistic Variation: The Case of Fraternity Men. *Journal of Sociolinguistics*, 2(1):69–99.

Kiesling, S. F. (2004). Dude. *American Speech*, 79(3):281–305.

Kiesling, S. F. (2011). *Linguistic Variation and Change*. Edinburgh University Press, Edinburgh.

Labov, W. (1963). The Social Motivation of a Sound Change. *Word*, 19:273–309.

Labov, W. (1966). *The Social Stratification of English in New York City*. Center for Applied Linguistics, Washington, DC.

Labov, W. (1990). The Intersection of Sex and Social Class in the Course of Linguistic Change. *Language Variation and Change*, 2(2):205–254.

Labov, W. (2001). *Principles of Linguistic Change. Vol. 2: Social Factors*. Blackwell Publishers, Oxford.

Lambert, W., Hodgson, R., Gardner, R., and Fillenbaum, S. (1960). Evaluational Reactions to Spoken Language. *Journal of Abnormal and Social Psychology*, 60(1):44–51.

Lanning, S. (2015). *A Gay/Straight Comparison of Gay Voices*. MA thesis, Ball State University, Muncie, IN.

Linville, S. E. (1998). Acoustic Correlates of Perceived Versus Actual Sexual Orientation in Men's Speech. *Folia Phoniatrica et Logopaedica*, 50(1), 35–48.

McGurk, H. and Macdonald, J. (1976). Hearing Lips and Seeing Voices. *Nature*, 264(5588):746–748.

Miller, L. (2004). Those Naughty Teenage Girls: Japanese Kogals, Slang, and Media Assessments. *Journal of Linguistic Anthropology*, 14(2):225–247.

Milroy, L. (1980). *Language and Social Networks*. Blackwell, Malden, MA.

Munson, B. (2007). The Acoustic Correlates of Perceived Masculinity, Perceived Femininity, and Perceived Sexual Orientation. *Language and Speech*, 50(1):125–142.

Namy, L. L., Nygaard, L. C., and Sauerteig, D. (2002). Gender Differences in Vocal Accommodation: The Role of Perception. *Journal of Language and Social Psychology*, 21(4):422–432.

Nevalainen, T. and Raumolin-Brunberg, H. (2016). *Historical Sociolinguistics: Language Change in Tudor and Stuart England*. Routledge, New York, NY.

Niedzielski, N. (1999). The Effect of Social Information on the Perception of Sociolinguistic Variables. *Journal of Language and Social Psychology*, 18(1):62–85.

Ochs, E. (1992). Indexing Gender. In Duranti, A. and Goodwin, C., editors, *Rethinking Context*, pages 335–358. Cambridge University Press, New York, NY.

Pardo, J. S. (2006). On Phonetic Convergence During Conversational Interaction. *Journal of the Acoustical Society of America*, 119(4):2382–2393.

Podesva, R. J. (2007). Phonation Type as a Stylistic Variable: The Use of Falsetto in Constructing a Persona. *Journal of Sociolinguistics*, 11(4):478–504.

Podesva, R. J. (2011). The California Vowel Shift and Gay Identity. *American Speech*, 86(1):32–51.

Poplack, S. (1980). The Notion of the Plural in Puerto Rican Spanish: Competing Constraints on (s) Deletion. In Labov, W., editor, *Locating Language in Time and Space*, pages 55–66. Academic Press, New York, NY

Sankoff, D. and Laberge, S. (1978). The Linguistic Market and the Statistical Explanation of Variability. In Sankoff, D., editor, *Linguistic Variation: Models and Methods*, pages 239–250. Academic Press, New York, NY.

Sidnell, J. (1999). Gender and Pronominal Variation in an Indo-Guyanese Creole-Speaking Community. *Language in Society*, 28(3):367–399.

Smyth, R., Jacobs, G., and Rogers, H. (2003). Male Voices and Perceived Sexual Orientation: An Experimental and Theoretical Approach. *Language in Society*, 32(3):329–350.

Strand, E. A. (2000). *Gender Stereotype Effects in Speech Processing*. PhD dissertation, Ohio State University, Columbus, OH.

Strand, E. A. and Johnson, K. (1996). Gradient and Visual Speaker Normalization in the Perception of Fricatives. In *Natural Language Processing and Speech Technology, Results of the 3rd KONVENS Conference, Bielefeld, Germany, October 1996*, pages 14–26.

Trudgill, P. (1972). Sex, Covert Prestige and Linguistic Change in the Urban British English of Norwich. *Language in Society*, 1(2):179–195.

Zimman, L. (2014). Transmasculinity and the Voice: Gender Assignment, Identity, and Presentation. In Milani, T., editor, *Language and Masculinities: Performances, Intersections, Dislocations*, pages 197–219. Routledge, New York, NY.

Zimman, L. (2017). Variability in /s/ Among Transgender Speakers: Evidence for a Socially Grounded Account of Gender and Sibilants. *Linguistics*; 55(5):993–1019.

Chapter 8

Putting it all together

Gender, sexuality, and language infuse life and society

This book is a beginning, and not complete, because there's a huge amount of research that I have left out. But a short textbook is necessarily selective, so my goal has been to give you an idea of all the ways that language and gender/sexuality impact, and are impacted by, language. As I hope you know by now, the relationship of language to gender and sexuality is not one-way, or even two-way. Rather, the manner in which language influences gender/sexuality can in turn influence language again, having new effects. For example, recall the calls to physicians' offices that Kitzinger (2005a,b) analyzes, discussed in Chapter 5. The first thing that the person answering the phone hears is a voice that gives cues about gender. Not only pitch, but perhaps even clues about what kind of man or woman is calling (class, age, race, among other things). As we've seen in the last chapter, these categorizations then change the way further language is heard. So before very much happens (that is, not long after "Hello!"), gender and other social identities have been categorized by the speakers. These categories are probably influenced by the kinds of labels that people have for social identities, even down to simple age categories such as woman versus girl or man versus boy: If a young-sounding woman calls, the answerer might call her a *girl*, whereas for the same-aged masculine voice, they would probably not call him a *boy*, but perhaps a *young man*.

Going forward in such a conversation, everything is now heard in a particular way because of the perceived identity of the speaker and this perceived identity affects the other kinds of categories expected. If the caller is a woman, the person who answers the phone might expect more politeness, or a certain kind of politeness, from the speaker (and those expectations might depend on *their* gender). In addition, they might be friendlier to a woman if she uses less 'vernacular' speech, but friendlier to a man if he uses more 'vernacular' speech. And as we saw in Chapter 5, our perceptions of a person's gender affect expectations about sexual identity as well. The person answering, having heard a feminine voice, will likely not expect to hear talk about the caller's wife, for example. So, even though I discussed categorization, interaction, and pronunciation in different chapters, they are not independent of one another by any means.

To recap, language helps to create gender categories and ideologies, it influences how we interact with each other, and it influences our accent and how we hear accents. What emerges is a picture of gender as a pervasive perceptual category that organizes how we think about humans, but one that is not organized universally across humanity (although it does seem to be a universal that all cultures have some notion of gender categorization and ideologies about gender and sexuality). And language is a central part aspect of the ways that gender/sexuality variability is performed, created, and even policed.

Taken together, the studies discussed in this book give us an overall picture of the interactions of language, gender, and sexuality. Most important are the ideologies about gender and sexuality that circulate in communities and cultures: What does it mean to be *masculine* or *feminine*? How divided are those categories and what are the consequences of not conforming to the categories? Language ties into those stereotypes in many ways, as we have seen throughout the book. Words refer to different categories, and those categories are used by speakers to identify different kinds of masculinity and femininity. Language is also used to define or 'recreate' those relationships as we apply them talking to each other. Categorization is also important for social institutions such as marriage, and labels about people such as *women* and *men*. And language structures not only how people talk about these categories, but also how those categories fit into our expectations about sexuality and intimacy, with some kinds of language reflecting assumptions about unmarked sexual and intimate relations, and displaying those that a community finds marked.

At the same time, these gender ideologies structure the ways that people talk, both in terms of interaction and things like politeness and stancetaking, and in terms of accents, grammar use, and word choice. These kinds of differences, structured by gender, are importantly not **categorical**. So, if you started this book and hoped to be able to explain to people at the end that women speak one way and men another, you'll be disappointed. There are **statistical** patterns of use for feminine and masculine people, but these are not categorical. I stress this point because it's easy to forget and humans like to make categorical generalizations: There's more variability *within* gender categories than *between* them in language patterns (and almost everything else too). This is even more visible when we look at sexuality, where in English we find the **enregistered** way of speaking that some people call the 'gay voice.' But this voice is not used categorically by all gay men; it is part of a social presentation – or, more accurately, a performance in the way Butler uses the term, an indexical connection to a particular, culturally recognizable, identity category.

We have explored many different ways that language 'patterns' by gender: Patterns of accent, grammar, word choice, and interaction. What is the explanation for these patterns? This is the Big Question when it comes to language, gender, and sexuality: The Explanation. Any particular pattern or set of patterns needs to be related to the ways they are used to do the performative work of identity. In other words, are they initially simply being used to signal an identity? For example, am I swearing a lot because I want to seem masculine or am I doing something else? Maybe a little of both. I don't swear all the time, so it's not some automatic function of wanting to be perceived as masculine all the time. I'm more likely to swear to show different kinds of stances I'm taking. How exactly that works depends on the particular situation and the terms being used, but the point is that the swearing has a function beyond just indexing masculinity, and the other indexicalities of swearing likely connect with masculinity, such as 'roughness' or even simply not being polite.

What I just described is a version of the **indirect indexicality** that has been an important theoretical concept throughout the book. It's a good rubric for thinking about the ways that gender stereotypes are related to how femininity and masculinity are performed and recognized through language. It's the difference between saying "women are more polite" and "women are expected to do things with more politeness and refinement because of stereotypes of femininity." The second version is longer and not as easy to say, or even explain, but the first makes the mistake of suggesting that women are somehow inherently more polite than men, which is not true. So stances are ideologically and sometime stereotypically connected to masculinity and femininity (or other more specific gendered identities such as sexual identities or more specific kinds of gender/sexual identities such as the 'gay diva' discussed by Podesva [2007]). People recognize that language users are taking stances with their language and then connect those ways of speaking to those kinds of identities.

Although the figure showing this relationship in Chapter 4 has nice neat arrows and lines, that's really just to get the idea of how it works. In reality, things are not just more complicated, but messier, in the sense that there aren't clear arrows going in a clear direction, but indexical meanings are exploding and reverberating. For example, if a speaker is recognized as a masculine person, and addresses a feminine person with politeness or courtesy, this might be perceived as 'chivalry,' with all the historical baggage that brings in. So, while we can make these abstract arrows and categories as in Ochs' figure, we really only know what is going on when we are looking at an actual interaction in an actual community. In addition, sometimes people have multiple meanings and multiple agendas, and they can't articulate their meanings. Before you get too frustrated, my point here is that interaction and language are inherently multifunctional and often vague, and rely on the listener to really, well, listen. If you are frustrated by all this fuzziness, just remember that this aspect of language is also what gives us a lot of humor, poetry, literature, and other genres that rely on and celebrate the multitude of meaning potentials in any one utterance. And it doesn't mean we can't make generalizations about gender/sexuality and language, just that we have to be careful in how we do that.

Note above that I said that someone might want to be perceived as being masculine (or feminine, or some other specific identity). One aspect of language, gender, and sexuality that hasn't been explored much is the **motivation** behind wanting to be perceived in a particular way. How is it that we develop our identities such that we want to be perceived as being more feminine, or masculine, or gay, or non-binary? Such questions are generally those of psychology, but there's a place for language and gender to investigate the interactions in young kids and families to see how the desire to become a particular kind of person develops. While we've seen some research on kids (Goodwin 1990; Ochs and Schieffelin 1995), there's a lot to explore in this topic, especially with respect to very young children (see, for example, Sheldon 1990, 1996).

The other part of "want to be perceived" is "perceived." Gender/sexuality in language is something that is performed, but that means that it also has to be recognized. We've seen, especially in Chapter 7, that the perception of indexicality is also complex. For example, a *walkin'* pronunciation does not always have the same indexicality, and as noted above, politeness might be seen as chivalry and thus masculine rather than feminine. So the perception of language as gendered also changes depending on the situation and the listener. We can imagine that a particular way of speaking, such as a 'Valley Girl' style with rising intonation, prodigious use of *like*, glottal stop replacement for /t/, and California vowels, indexes that particular persona. But what if one of those features is used by a much older woman (say of the 'Baby Boom' generation)? It's unlikely that we'll recognize it as 'Valley Girl' persona unless we understand her to be performing a type of person she isn't (such as if she is making fun of the stereotype). Meaning is much more than decoding a sound, especially indexical meaning (recall the discussion of Campbell-Kibler [2008], with some speakers being annoying and others not depending on their accent).

So, hopefully you now have an idea of the complexities of the intersection of language, gender, and sexuality, but also appreciate the intricate ways that meanings are built in communities and in interactions. The richness and creativity of meaning that human language expresses beyond the 'dictionary definitions' of words can sometimes be frustrating, but it is ultimately another tool that allows us to have such marvelously complex social lives. Moreover, we can't simply carve out gender and sexuality away from the context, especially other social identities that affect language and that people use language to perform. We can only go so far in talking about a feminine person before we realize that our unmarked feminine person is, for example, White and middle class.

I said above that I had to leave a lot out. I've already mentioned a few things in this chapter, but you're probably wondering what else I might have left out. There's a lot to explore in how language is used in particular domains, and a significant one is the workplace. While there have been some sociolinguistic studies in this area (for example, Tannen 1995; Holmes and Stubbe 2015; Angouri 2018), a lot of what you might read is geared toward telling women what they are doing wrong rather than more sensitively analyzing why people believe women (and not men) need to change their behavior. In short, there's still a lot of work to do. Other domains include the legal domain and the medical domain. There's also still lots to do about gender in different kinds of families and about kids of all ages. I hope some of you are inspired to wonder, for example, how talk in the medical setting is different from the generalizations you've learned about in this book, or how and why kids learn to speak in more masculine or feminine ways.

There are also some new directions that research is headed in that I haven't talked about a lot, because there isn't a lot to talk about. The research on Trans identities is still in its infancy but reveals much about the performative nature of gender/sexuality and language (among other issues about gender and sexuality). Also incipient in this subfield is the understanding of the manner in which people who variously identify as Trans use language to help them create that identity; the research so far (such as Zimman 2014) makes clear that it is far more complex than using 'women's language' or 'men's language' for the 'target' gender identity.

The study of Trans-identified people relates to another important trend in language and gender/sexuality studies, namely how the use of language is related to physicality, both the ways bodies and language are used together and how language helps to structure the physical. The connection between Trans-identified people and bodies was noted earlier, as was the connection between gesture and body (the discussion of head cant by Voigt et al. [2016] in Chapter 6). This kind of research is just beginning, especially with the rise of powerful new computational tools for linking language and video. Physicality is also important in areas where there is disembodiment, namely in electronic communication. These modes of communication are always changing and the ways they interact with gender and sexuality are also always changing. One big question is the extent to which electronic communication affects the spoken – what forms are taken into the spoken language and used, and is that related to gender and sexuality at all?

Finally, we are starting to come to terms with some of the 'fuzziest' notions that relate to gender/sexuality and language, which are the realms related to emotion, affect, feelings, and so on. I've claimed (Kiesling 2018) that feelings are related to gender and sexual identity. It's not so much that gender ideologies, for example, suggest that men should not show emotion, but that masculinity and femininity project into the world different ways of feeling. In this context, my argument has been that in the US, masculinity is related to a recognizable feeling of 'masculine ease,' and that we can find particular forms of language and stances that create this ease. All of these areas are still at the beginning of a research program, but they all tell us something about how language creates and reflects gender and sexuality, and, at the same time, how language is influenced and changed by sexuality and gender.

References

Angouri, J. (2018). *Culture, Discourse, and the Workplace.* Routledge, New York, NY.

Campbell-Kibler, K. (2008). I'll be the Judge of That: Diversity in Social Perceptions of (ING). *Language in Society*, 37(5):637–659.

Goodwin, M. H. (1990). *He-Said-She-Said: Talk as Social Organization Among Black Children.* Indiana University Press, Bloomington, IN.

Holmes, J. and Stubbe, M. (2015). *Power and Politeness in the Workplace: A Sociolinguistic Analysis of Talk at Work.* Routledge, New York, NY.

Kiesling, S. (2018). Masculine Stances and the Linguistics of Affect: On Masculine Ease. *NORMA*, 13(3–4):191–212.

Kitzinger, C. (2005a). Heteronormativity in Action: Reproducing the Heterosexual Nuclear Family in After-Hours Medical Calls. *Social Problems*, 52(4):477–498.

Kitzinger, C. (2005b). "Speaking as a Heterosexual": (How) Does Sexuality Matter for Talk-in-Interaction? *Research on Language & Social Interaction*, 38(3):221–265.

Ochs, E. and Schieffelin, B. (1995). Language Acquisition and Socialization: Three Developmental Stories and Their Implications. In Blount, B. G., editor, *Language, Culture, and Society*, pages 470–512. Waveland Press, Prospect Heights, IL.

Podesva, R. J. (2007). Phonation Type as a Stylistic Variable: The Use of Falsetto in Constructing a Persona. *Journal of Sociolinguistics*, 11(4):478–504.

Sheldon, A. (1990). Pickle Fights: Gendered Talk in Preschool Disputes. *Discourse Processes*, 13(1):5–31.

Sheldon, A. (1996). You Can be the Baby Brother, But You Aren't Born Yet: Preschool Girls' Negotiation for Power and Access in Pretend Play. *Research on Language & Social Interaction*, 29(1):57–80.

Tannen, D. (1995). *Talking From 9 to 5: Women and Men in the Workplace*. Harper, New York, NY.

Voigt, R., Eckert, P., Jurafsky, D., and Podesva, R. J. (2016). Cans and Cants: Computational Potentials for Multimodality With a Case Study. *Journal of Sociolinguistics*, 20(5):677–711.

Zimman, L. (2014). The Discursive Construction of Sex: Remaking and Reclaiming the Gendered Body in Talk About Genitals Among Trans Men. In Zimman, L., Davis, J., and Raclaw, J., editors, *Queer Excursions: Retheorizing Binaries in Language, Gender, and Sexuality*, pages 13–34. Oxford University Press, New York, NY.

Index